Creative Crafts for Creative Hands

MAKING
HOME ACCESSORIES

CLB 4130
This edition published in 1995 by Tiger Books International PLC, London
© 1995 CLB Publishing, Godalming, Surrey
Printed and bound in Proost, N.V. Belgium
All rights reserved
ISBN 1-85501-595-1

Managing Editor: Jo Finnis
Editors: Sue Wilkinson; Geraldine Christy
Jacket and prelim design: Art of Design
Typesetting: Litho Link Ltd, Welshpool, Powys
Production: Ruth Arthur; Sally Connolly; Neil Randles; Karen Staff; Jonathan Tickner; Matthew Dale
Director of Production: Gerald Hughes

Photographers
Jacket John Suett/Eaglemoss; Jacket flap Graham Rae/ Eaglemoss; Title page Steve Tanner/ Eaglemoss; 9 Graham Rae/Eaglemoss; 10 Simon Page-Ritchie/ Eaglemoss; 13 Ariadne Holland; 14 Ariadne Holland; 15-16 Steve Tanner/ Eaglemoss; 17 Ariadne Holland; 19 (tl) Simon Page-Ritchie/Eaglemoss; 19 (br) Steve Tanner/Eaglemoss; 21 Steve Tanner/Eaglemoss; 23 Steve Tanner/Eaglemoss; 25-26 Steve Tanner/Eaglemoss; 27-29 Steve Tanner/Eaglemoss; 30 (tl) Steve Tanner/ Eaglemoss; 30 (tr) VMP Redaktionsservice; 30 (br) Steve Tanner/Eaglemoss; 31-34 Graham Rae/Eaglemoss; 35-36 Graham Rae/Eaglemoss; 37-38 Steve Tanner/Eaglemoss; 39-42 Graham Rae/Eaglemoss; 43-44 Simon Page-Ritchie/ Eaglemoss; 45-46 Steve Tanner/ Eaglemoss; 47 John Suett/ Eaglemoss; 48 Sue Atkinson/ Eaglemoss; 49-52 Steve Tanner/Eaglemoss; 53-54 John Suett/Eaglemoss; 55 (tl) Mal Stone/Eaglemoss; 55 (br) Steve Tanner/Eaglemoss; 56 Steve Tanner/ Eaglemoss; 57-58 Graham Rae/Eaglemoss; 59 Steve Tanner/Eaglemoss; 60 Steve Tanner/ Eaglemoss.

Illustrators
10-12 Tig Sutton; 16 Terry Evans; 18 Terry Evans; 20 Terry Evans; 22-24 Kate Simunek ; 26 Kate Simunek; 28-30 John Hutchinson; 32-34 Kate Simunek; 36 Kate Simunek; 40-42 Kate Simunek; 44 Kate Simunek; 46 Terry Evans; 48 Christine Hart-Davies; 50-52 John Hutchinson; 54 Kate Simunek; 56 John Hutchinson; 58 Kate Simunek; 60 Kate Simunek.

Creative Crafts for Creative Hands

M A K I N G

HOME ACCESSORIES

*How to make beautiful gifts and objects for the home,
from basic techniques to finishing touches.*

**TIGER BOOKS INTERNATIONAL
LONDON**

Contents

Candle lampshades   9

Painted tulip napkins   13

Napkin ties   15

Pretty storage boxes   17

Decorative shelf edgings   19

Colourful hooked rug   21

Shell picture frame   25

Fabric roses   27

Ribbon rose cushions   31

A dough basket   35

Cover story   37

Coffee pot cosies   39

Decorating trays   43

Seasonal tie-backs   45

Lace-framed pot pourri   47

Table-top tidies   49

Basket bows   53

Fabric-covered plates   55

Treasure troves   57

Painted pottery   59

Candle lampshades

Candles covered with decorative card or fabric shades are very much in vogue at the moment. There is almost always a drawer full of unused candles somewhere in the home, usually kept at hand in case of a power cut. And just about any candlestick can be transformed into a pretty lamp. All you need are shade carriers, straight-sided candles and the shade materials.

The shades themselves are very easy to make and the same shades can be used on electric candle lamps provided you use the appropriate carrier. They will look charming on a dining table, or alternatively add an extremely appealing touch to the top of a cupboard, a chest of drawers or the mantle over a fireplace. You might even take the idea and turn it into a special feature or conversation piece in your home by making several different types and displaying them in every room. You should never leave burning candles unattended as the shades are only made from card or fabric, but this shouldn't be a problem as these lovely candle lamps look just as attractive, unlit.

Choose a style of shade to suit the candlestick itself as well as the decor of the room. A plain or cut glass candlestick might be enhanced by a delicate pink shade, a pale blue one, or a plain one covered with splashes of gold. Plain brown paper or parchment shades would complement the more ethnic, wooden style of decoration, while shades decorated with chic tartans, gold stars or ribbons and bows would look terrific in a more formal room.

You can have a lot of fun experimenting with different coloured card and fabrics. Try altering the shape of the edging too, by cutting points instead of scallops for example. Another eye-catching variation could be produced by letting the light through tiny perforations or shapes cut out from the surface of the shade.

The lampshade carriers can be bought from most good interior design or lighting suppliers, and most good lighting stores should be able to order one for you.

▶ Natural light
It is possible to create atmosphere using the most unsophisticated materials. This parchment and raffia shade with its verdigris candlestick is perfectly set off by the rough-textured wall.

Making candle lampshades

The different materials used will suit varying styles of interior decoration. The following suggestions are not exhaustive but offer a range of possibilities from the very simple and natural, to the more detailed and ornate styles. Once you start experimenting, you will probably come up with more ideas.

A PARCHMENT SHADE

Materials

Lampshade carrier
Parchment 40 x 20cm (16 x 8in) from craft shops or specialist paper shops
Strands of raffia or **laces** for the top and bottom
Eyelet machine or small **hole punch**
Clear adhesive

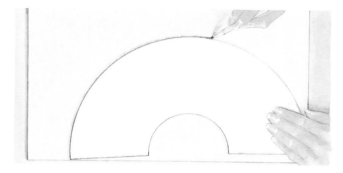

1 Cutting the shape Follow the instructions for the template as described overleaf. Draw around the template on the parchment and cut out the shape.

▲ **Shady character** Three very different lampshade styles are depicted here – choose one that best suits the style of your room.

2 Punching holes Before making holes in the parchment, use a pencil to mark the hole positions about 4cm (1½in) apart, 1cm (⅜in) in from the top and bottom edges. Use a hole punch or eyelet machine, to make the small holes all the way round the top and bottom.

3 Making up the shade Apply clear adhesive along the overlapping edge and stick the two side edges together. Press together firmly and then leave shade to dry.

4 Adding raffia decoration Thread the raffia through the holes, looping it around the edge. Secure by tying raffia in a decorative knot at the front or glue it down neatly.

5 Securing the shade Position the shade over the metal carrier and carefully push it over the top edge until the shade slots firmly into place. The rim of the shade should fit quite tightly around the brass rim of the carrier. It is important to fit the shade to the carrier before placing the whole thing over your candle.

FIRE SAFETY

A word of warning As the candle lampshades are only made out of card, paper or fabric, the manufacturer's instructions for the carrier must be adhered to. Never leave burning candles unattended. Only use straight-sided candles, 2cm (¾in) in diameter. Never let candles burn lower than 10cm (4in). Before lighting, make sure the carrier sits straight on the candle and the card shade fits snugly over the top.

A FABRIC-COVERED SHADE

Materials
Lampshade carrier
Medium card
Fabric strip, 40 x 20cm (16 x 8in)
Iron-on bonding web (one packet will make three shades)
Fine black cord, 1m (39½in)

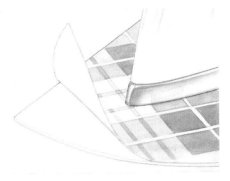

1 Cutting out the shape Make a template from thick card using the pattern and instructions as before. Use the template to cut out the shade from medium card, bonding web and fabric. When cutting out the fabric shape, it is important to make sure that the centre of the template is placed along the straight grain of the fabric.

2 Bonding the fabric Iron the bonding web, paper side facing upwards, on to the card. Remove the paper covering from the bonding web, then place the fabric on top, right side up. Iron to bond the materials together.

3 Making up the shade Run a fine line of clear adhesive along the seam and stick together as before. To neaten the top and bottom edges, run a fine line of adhesive around each edge and stick a decorative cord trim in place. Trim to fit at join.

A STENCILLED SHADE

Materials
White or colour card
Ready cut star stencil
Stencil paint
Clean, dry **stencil brush**
Paper or **kitchen towel**
Spray adhesive
Narrow gold cord

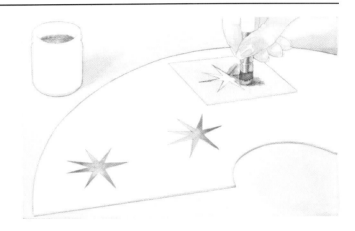

1 Preparing the shade Using a template, cut out the lampshade from the card as before. Then mark the positions of the stars with a pencil. Secure your stencil using spray adhesive.

Alternative stars
If you have difficulty stencilling the stars evenly or without smudging the paint, you could try drawing the star shapes on to the back of gold paper using the stencil. Then cut them out with sharp pointed scissors and stick them directly on to the shade using spray adhesive.

2 Stencilling the design Take the stencil brush and dip just the tips of the bristles into the stencil paint. Dab the brush on to a wad of paper towel to distribute the paint evenly on the brush and to dry the paint slightly. Then dab the paint-covered brush or apply in a circling motion to your stencil, to form the star shape. You should use as little paint as possible to prevent smudging. As each star dries, peel off the stencil, clean off the paint before repeating the process to paint the remaining stars.

3 Making up Glue the two ends of the shade together and trim with matching cord as before.

A WALLPAPER SHADE

Materials
Wallpaper strip 40 x 20cm (16 x 8in)
Medium card
Wire-edged ribbon
Spray adhesive

1 Lining the shade Unless the wallpaper is very firm it is best to stiffen it with card. Using the template, cut out shades from wallpaper and from card. Bond together with spray adhesive. Mark scallops along the lower edge and cut out with scissors. Make up as before.

2 Decorating with bows Mark the shade into quarters and stick the strips of ribbon in position. Fold the cut ends to the inside at the top. Stick firmly in place. Make the four bows and stick them to the strips of ribbon along the lower edge. Pull the bows out into full bow shapes. This should be particularly easy with the wire-edged ribbon which ensures that the bows don't droop.

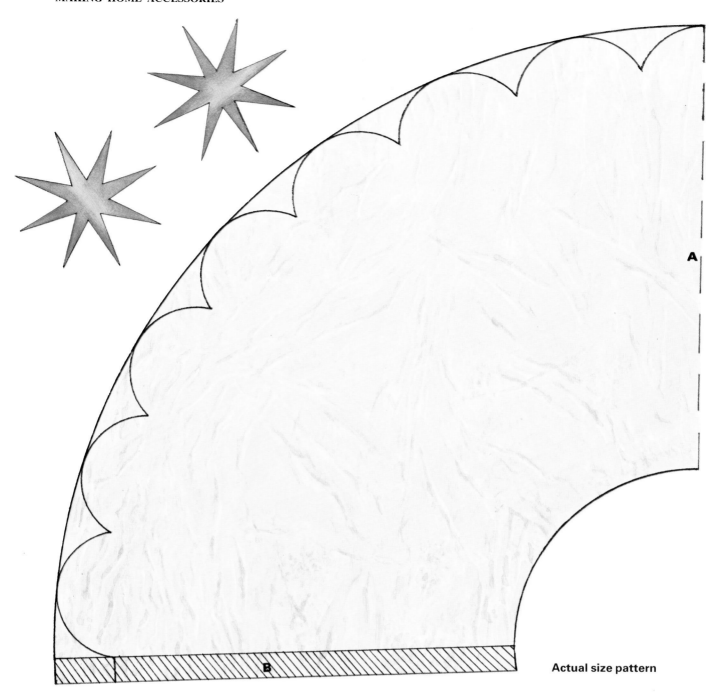

A

B

Actual size pattern

A LAMPSHADE PATTERN

Materials
Tracing paper
Thick card
Sharp scissors
Clear adhesive

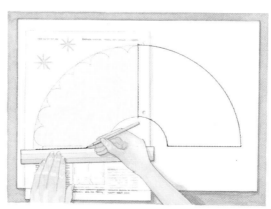

1 **Tracing the pattern** Draw a centre line. Match it to line (**A**) on the pattern above and trace off left side. Turn over the paper and repeat for right side. Add shaded area (**B**) to the left side.

▲ *Pattern for lampshade* *Use this for each design.*

2 **Making the template** Transfer the design from the tracing paper to thick card and cut out the template using sharp scissors.

3 **Checking the fit** Cut out the tracing paper pattern. Stick the ends together, covering the shaded area with glue. Push over the top of the brass carrier. The shade should fit snugly and hold firmly in place.

Painted tulip napkins

Painting motifs on to fabric, then working simple embroidery stitches over them is a pretty way of making your table napkins totally original. Use this tulip motif or choose a favourite flower and paint it on a plain napkin, adding embroidery stitches to highlight or define the design. Motifs could also be painted on to other soft furnishings – cushion covers, table or tray cloths.

Materials
Plain purchased napkin
Colourfast fabric paint, one jar in each of Malachite Green, Red and White
Medium paintbrush
Stranded cotton one skein each jade, pink and sand
Crewel embroidery needle
Dressmaker's carbon paper

▲ **Freshly painted**
These simple tulips have been painted using a few bold strokes of colour. Use the template as a guide, starting with a pale wash and adding a darker shade to outline the shapes. On a set of napkins, vary the motifs using the single flower on some, double on others.

13

TO WORK THE MOTIF

1 Transfer the design Trace the tulip on to the napkin using dressmaker's carbon paper.

2 Paint the tulip Using white paint mixed with red and green to achieve different shades, paint the flower following the traced outline. Before painting the napkin, practise on paper to work out the effect you wish to achieve. Leave to dry, then fix the design on the fabric following the maker's instructions.

3 Embroider the motif Using two strands of embroidery cotton work stem stitch to outline parts of the design in stem stitch, following the bold lines on the pattern. Use pink for the tulip head and sand and jade for leaves and stem.

4 Adding texture Using two strands of pink, work filling stitches on the tulip heads following the fine lines on the design.

5 Embroider the edge Using two strands of pink work chain stitch around the napkin, along the hem.

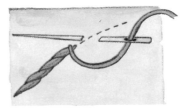

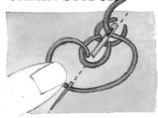

STEM STITCH

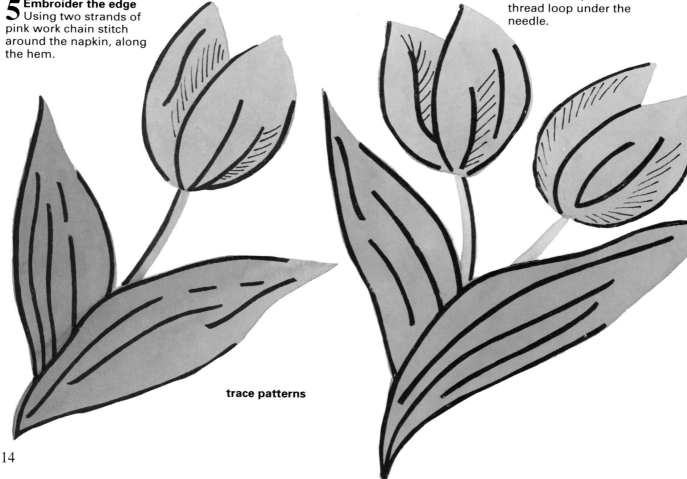

Working from left to right along the line of the design, bring the needle up through the fabric. Insert the needle to the right, angling it to emerge half a stitch length back.

CHAIN STITCH

Working from right to left, bring the needle up through the fabric. Holding the thread in a loop with your thumb, insert the needle at almost the same place. Bring it out a stitch length away, along the line to be embroidered, with the thread loop under the needle.

trace patterns

Napkin ties

Smart napkin ties are a must for meal times and these cheerful checked rings definitely fit the bill. Stiffened to hold their shape the different tartan plaids are mixed and matched, then tied into interesting knots, to make each one different. No stitching is needed, you simply cut and stick, so they're really quick to make.

Each napkin ring is made from a strip of fabric liberally dipped in adhesive then wound and moulded into shape. When the adhesive dries it hardens, giving the rings a solid appearance as well as adding an all-over sheen.

All the materials you need can be found in the home – the adhesive is a

▲ Colourful rings
These bright and cheerful breakfast companions will gladden the early morning table. If you make a different ring for each person they'll be instantly recognisable.

PVA and the fabric rings can be moulded round an old cardboard tube from the inside of a kitchen towel roll. The adhesive is mixed with water to the consistency of single cream and even though it has a cloudy effect on the fabric it will dry clear.

Choose a bright cheerful fabric that looks good with your china as well as the kitchen decor.

Materials
Fabrics a selection of colour co-ordinating, plain, checks or flowered fabrics to mix and match, so that each design of napkin ring can be made slightly different

Cling film or **plastic bag**

Kitchen foil

Cardboard tube from kitchen towel roll

Clear adhesive tape

Sharp scissors, rust-proof pins and a **tape measure**

PVA adhesive

Basin and an **old spoon** for mixing the PVA adhesive

Paint brush

Ribbon rosebuds

NAPKINS WITH BOWS

TWISTED AND DRAPED BOW

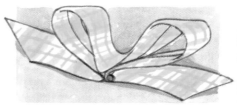

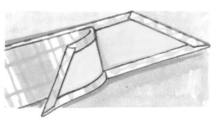

How to stiffen the fabric

Mix two parts water with eight parts PVA adhesive and stir well. Pass the fabric strips through the adhesive pushing it down into the liquid with a paint brush, keeping the strips flat. Remove each strip and run it through your fingers to remove excess adhesive.

Cover the cardboard tube with cling film or plastic, sticking in place with adhesive tape. Push ends of film down inside the tube. Then mould napkin tie into shape; pin to hold. Leave to dry overnight.

1 Making bows Make up a basic napkin ring see *Rosebud Ring*, using a striped fabric. For bow, cut a strip of checked fabric 76 x 14cm (30 x 5½in). Fold in half lengthways and cut diagonally across each end. Unfold and press in 1cm (⅜in) on all edges, then press the whole strip in half. Run the strip through the adhesive keeping edges together. Form the strip into a bow shape with two loops and ties, pin to hold.

1 Sorting the fabrics Cut one piece of small check fabric and one of large check fabric each 70 x 10cm (27½ x 4in). Place together and cut diagonally across ends. Press in 1cm (⅜in) all round each piece. Pass both strips through PVA, as before. Place strips wrong sides together exactly matching outer edges.

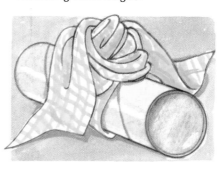

ROSEBUD RING

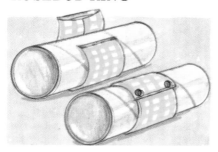

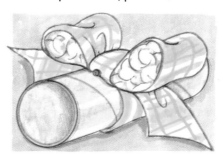

2 Finishing off For bow centre, cut one piece 24 x 4.5cm (9½ x 1¾in). Press in all edges for 1cm (⅜in). Stick the bow shape on top of the napkin ring. Dip the bow centre in adhesive and wind round the centre of bow and napkin ring, pulling the bow into shape and holding it in place on the fabric ring; pin to hold. Stuff the bow loops with loosely scrunched-up balls of foil and leave to dry. Then remove foil and pins.

2 Making the ring Place the card tube centrally on the strip. Bring the strip ends firmly round the tube and twist them together twice where they meet at the top. Make sure the knot is firm, and pin if necessary. Drape loose ends over the napkin ring as shown. Make sure the two fabrics stay firmly together. Leave to dry.

1 Making the ring Cut a length of fabric 23 x 19cm (9 x 7½in). Press 1cm (⅜in) to wrong side all round, then press long edges to the middle of wrong side. Drag through PVA and shape round tube, overlapping short ends at base; pin to tube. Pinch fabric edges together at top and pin.

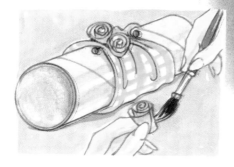

2 Adding rosebuds When dry, use the neat PVA and a paint brush to stick the ribbon rosebuds and leaves in place on the top. Finally twist the ring off the cardboard tube.

Pretty storage boxes

Use favourite fabric scraps and discarded boxes to bring order to your home by making some colourful stacking boxes. Covering boxes with fabrics is very easy, and by using materials that complement each other, the boxes can be placed on show to form an attractive and useful display.

Round or oval boxes are easier to cover than rectangular ones, and you can use hat boxes or gift boxes in a range of different sizes for stacking. Light to mediumweight fabrics are best for this project, but if you have a special embroidery, it can be displayed to great advantage when used to cover the box lid. Gorgeous gift paper can also be used, although it is less durable.

Usually the boxes look best with just the tailored fabric cover, but ribbons and trims can be added to the completed box to make it look more decorative. If you intend the boxes to be stored as a stack, remember to limit the decoration to the sides, where it can be shown off most effectively and will not be damaged beneath the other boxes.

Any size of box can be covered depending on what you wish to store. They are invaluable for organising your sewing materials, mementos or jewellery. In fact this could be the ideal

▲ Boxing clever
If you choose the box sizes and fabrics carefully you can make a lovely collection and display. Co-ordinate the fabric colours with the room, or use leftovers from furnishings for a perfect match.

opportunity to sort out the muddled contents of dressing-table drawers; put tights and stockings in one box, hair accessories in another, and stray make-up in a smaller one. Or colour co-ordinate your accessories, with green belts, socks and scarves in one, blue in another and red in a third.

17

Materials

Round or oval box with lid
Floral medium weight fabric large enough to cover the box and the inside and outside of the lid with extra to spare
Striped medium weight fabric for lining the inside of just the box (not the lid)
Spray adhesive
Sharp craft scissors
Old newspapers
Pencil
Fabric glue
Spray fabric protector
Tape measure and ruler

COVERING A BOX

1 **Preparing the fabric** Iron both the floral fabric and striped lining fabric to remove all the creases. Lay both fabrics flat on to the work surface with the wrong side up.

2 **Cutting out** Measure the circumference and the depth of the box side, add 2cm (1in) to both measurements and cut out a strip from both the floral and striped fabrics. Measure the circumference and depth of the lid sides, double the depth and add 2cm (1in) to both measurements, and cut out one strip from the floral fabric. Using the lid as a template, place it on the floral fabric and draw around it. Cut out the circle 1cm (½in) outside the drawn line. Then using this as a pattern piece, cut out two more in floral fabric and one in striped.

3 **Using the spray adhesive** Working in a well ventilated area or outside, cover a work area with old newspaper before using the adhesive. Spray fabric on the wrong side holding the can 15-20cm (6-8in) away from the work. Replace newspaper when it become tacky.

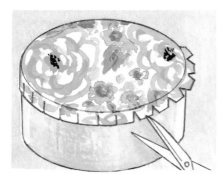

4 **Covering the base of the box** Spray adhesive over the wrong side of one floral fabric circle. Centre fabric on underside of box base; smooth out air bubbles. Snip evenly around edges to within 3mm (⅛in) of the box then fold and stick the snipped edge up the sides; to avoid bulk trim excess fabric where snipped tabs overlap.

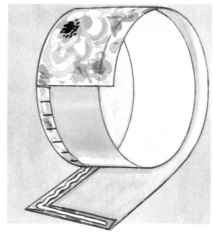

5 **Covering the sides** Spray the floral fabric strip for the box sides. Fold 1cm (½in) to wrong side along one long and one short edge, and run your thumb-nail along the folds. Lay it out flat on a clean work surface, right side down, then smear fabric glue over the wrong side of the fabric along these edges. With the box on its side and matching the folded edge of fabric to the lower edge of the box sides, wrap the strip around the box, lapping the folded end over the other end to neaten. Smooth out any air bubbles, then fold the fabric over the rim to the inside of the box, making sure that it is pressed firmly in place.

6 **Lining the box base** Spray striped fabric circle with adhesive and, centring the fabric, stick it to the inside of the box base. Check for air bubbles and run your thumb-nail around the inner edge.

7 **Lining the box sides** Snip the fluted edge of the striped inside circle at regular intervals and stick the snipped sections to the inner sides of the box. Trim 5mm (¼in) from the width of the striped fabric strip, then spray with adhesive. Fold 1cm (½in) to wrong side along both long edges and one short end. Run your thumb-nail along the folds, then smear fabric glue over the wrong side of these edges. Matching the one long folded edge to the lower edge of the box sides, stick the striped lining fabric to the inside of the box.

8 **Lining the lid** Using a floral fabric circle, cover the inside of the lid as for lining the box base.

9 **Covering the lid top** Using the last floral fabric circle, cover the box lid as for the base of the box.

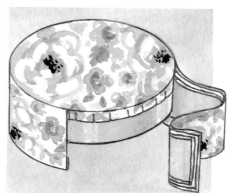

10 **Covering the lid sides** Spray adhesive over the wrong side of the last floral fabric strip. Turn 1cm (½in) to wrong side along both long edges and one short edge; crease and glue the edges as before. Matching one folded edge to the top of the lid, wrap the fabric around the lid. Fold the fabric over the lid edge and stick to the inside of the lid.

11 **Protecting the box** Following the manufacturers instructions, spray the fabric protector evenly all over the inside and the outside the box.

Decorative shelf edgings

Adding decorative shelf edgings is an easy and inexpensive way of brightening up the inside of a cupboard or a dull set of shelves. They can be used on any type of shelf unit, whether the shelves are always on display, half-hidden behind glass doors, or concealed in a cupboard.

Paper, fabric and many varieties of ribbons, braid and lace are all suitable for shelf edgings. To create different effects you can cover all the shelves with the same edging varying the colour or pattern on each shelf or produce a jubilant medley of styles, with perhaps paper on one shelf, and braid and lace on others. For good results match the style of the edgings with the items displayed on the shelves.

Depending on your style of decoration, and personal preference, shelf edgings can be as simple or as fancy as you wish. A length of shop-bought lace can give a rustic style, but for a more lively effect pleat braids and ribbons before attaching them. A length of wallpaper border can have an edge trimmed or a border can be cut from paper.

The best method of attaching the edging is by using double-sided sticky tape. This has the advantage of being invisible and easy to position. Cut a length of double-sided tape to match the width of the shelf and attach the sticky side to the shelf first. Remove the backing and press the edging firmly into place.

▲ Shelf style
This selection of shelf edgings includes a cut-out wallpaper border, lace and cut paper. The moiré green braid offers the simplest transformation.

'ANTIQUED' LACE

Materials

White cotton lace with a straight edge
Scissors
Tea and **hot water**
Shallow dish, preferably white so that you can see how the stain is progressing
Double-sided sticky tape

1 'Antique' the lace To create the colour and look of antique lace as shown here, soak a length of modern white cotton lace in tea before cutting it to size. The final shade depends on the strength of the tea and on the length of time you leave the lace soaking. The lace here was left in the tea for only two minutes.

2 Attach the edging Measure the shelf and cut the lace to fit. It should sit parallel with the top surface of the shelf, and not be stretched along the length, which might distort the pattern. Allow a little extra if you wish to turn under the ends to neaten and prevent the lace fraying.

CUT-OUT BORDERS

Materials

Wallpaper border of a suitable width
HB pencil
Sharp-pointed scissors
Double-sided sticky tape

Wallpaper border edgings can be trimmed along the bottom edge only or along both. Choose a design with a clearly-defined lower edge. Trailing stems or wispy lines are impossible to cut out.

1 Cut out the edging With the pencil, outline the side of the design which will eventually be your decorative edge. Leave the top edge straight and cut out the bottom edge, using sharp-pointed scissors removing the pencil marks as you cut.

PAPER CUT-OUTS

Materials

Paper – white till roll is a good width, but any fairly firm paper is suitable. Avoid foil papers or wallpaper, as they tend to crack when folded.
HB pencil and **stapler** (optional)
Sharp pointed scissors and **craft knife**
Cutting board
Double-sided sticky tape, sticky pads or **sticky tack**

These edgings are made on the same principle as the paper dolls cut out by children from a concertina of paper.

1 Cut out the paper Choose the edgings you wish to copy from our designs below, or experiment with your own designs. Cut a strip of paper to the correct width by the length of the shelf plus a little extra, which allows for centring the edging on the shelf.

2 Fold the concertina Measure and mark the width of your pattern on one end of the strip. For the 8cm (3¼in) deep square edging here, each folded section was 6cm (2¼in) wide. Make the first fold as accurately as possible, and fold up the remainder of the strip in concertina folds.

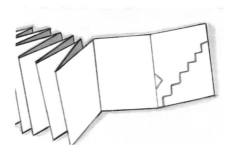

3 Mark out the design Copy your selected design, lining up the fold edges as marked. Draw the design on to the top section against the fold, on the wrong side of the paper. This is often easier if you unfold the first two flaps, but it is only necessary to draw the design on the first fold.

4 Cut out the pattern Before starting to cut, staple three folds together at a time on the areas that will be cut off. This will ensure that you cut accurately. It is difficult to cut through more than six sheets of paper and keep the pattern even. Using a pair of sharp-pointed scissors, cut around the edge of the design, cutting in from the edge on geometric designs.

5 Create complex patterns Use a craft knife to cut out intricate designs like **(c)** and **(d)** (left), where holes are cut out away from the folded edge, in the main part of the design.

6 Finish off Unfold the length of edging and press it flat with a cool iron between two sheets of paper before attaching it to the shelf. Any visible fold marks add to the naïve charm of the edging.

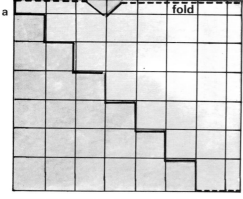

a   fold

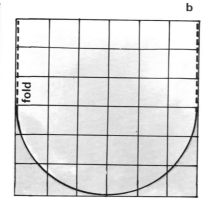

b

fold

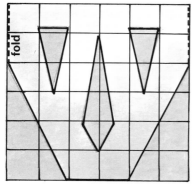

c   fold

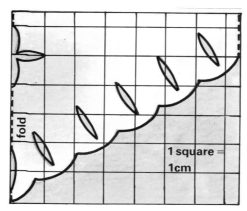

d   fold

1 square = 1cm

Colourful hooked rug

▲ Colourful combination
Brighten up a dull corner with this striking rug. The colour mix of dark pinks and purples set against a strong tartan background will look good against colour-washed walls and adds comfort to plain wooden floorboards.

This stunning rug combines two traditional motifs and designs. Large pink and purple roses are scattered across a warm tartan background. The result is a lovely rug that will be a pleasure to work and it will brighten up the darkest corner of any room.

The rug is worked across the canvas in rows, using a latchet hook and packs of cut wool lengths. Simply hook the lengths of wool through the firm canvas background, following the coloured chart overleaf, to make a sturdy and long-lasting rug. Two different methods of hooking are shown; try both and use the method you find easiest. The finished rug measures approximately 125 x 74cm (49 x 29in).

Materials

Rug canvas 127 x 76cm (50 x 30in) with 3 ⅓ holes to 2.5cm (1in)

6 ply pure new wool, 24 packs of dark purple, 14 packs of dark red, 13 packs of light pink, bright purple, medium pink and bright pink, 9 packs of light green, 8 packs of dark orange, 7 packs of light orange, 6 packs of dark green and 4 packs of white

Latchet rug hook

Sharp scissors

USING A LATCHET HOOK

There are basically two methods of hooking the knots which secure the wool to the canvas. Both methods are equally acceptable, but you must choose one and use it consistently for the whole rug, so that all the knots will lie in the same direction. Each method is easy to do, but if you have never made a rug, try both methods in one corner of the canvas before you begin, to discover which technique you prefer. These trial knots can be removed quickly.

Working together
When two people are working the rug together from opposite ends, one person must use Method 1 and the other Method 2, otherwise the pile will not lie in the same direction. If two people are working on the rug sitting side-by-side, they must both use the same method.

WORKING THE RUG

The rug is knotted across the canvas on the threads that run horizontally from selvedge edge to selvedge edge. Each square on the chart overleaf represents one knot. The chart shows half the design, which is turned round and repeated – apart from the centre row, which should only be worked once.

Method 1

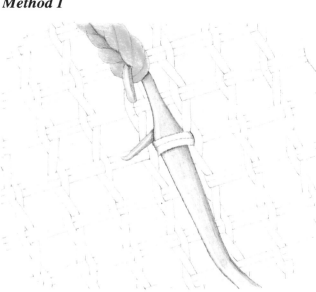

1 Begin the knot Push the hook under a double thread of canvas until the latchet part of the hook is through the canvas, then catch the loop of a folded piece of wool.

3 Pulling the wool ends Push the hook and latchet back through the loop of wool and catch the hook round both ends of the wool held in the fingers.

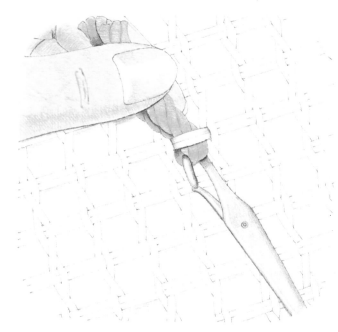

2 Forming a loop Carefully pull the hook slowly back through the canvas until the loop of wool comes under the canvas thread.

4 Tightening the knot Pull the hook back, bringing the wool ends through the loop. Pull lightly on the two ends of the yarn to tighten the knot.

Colourful hooked rug

1 **Beginning the rug** Lay the canvas on a table with the selvedges on either side. Place a weight on the canvas to stop it slipping. Fold up the first eight rows of canvas to the right side and, using your preferred method of knotting, work the first row of knots, following the chart for colours, through the double layers of canvas.

2 **Knotting the rug** Continue knotting, working the first eight rows through double canvas. Then work through single canvas, following the chart overleaf for colours. When the centre is reached, turn the chart round, matching A and B and work the second half. Always work in rows and in the same direction.

3 **Complete the hooking** When the last sixteen rows are reached, fold the canvas sharply along the line where the rug will end, and work the final rows through double thickness of canvas.

4 **Completing the rug** Turn under the selvedge edges and hand sew to back of rug. Give the rug a thorough rub in one direction with your hand to remove any loose fibres. Finally, trim any unusually long tufts with a sharp pair of scissors to achieve an even surface.

Method 2

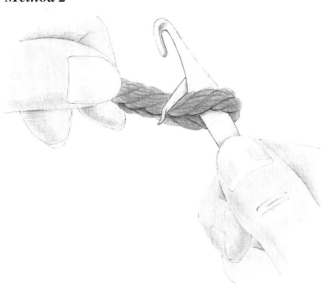

1 **Making the loop** Fold one length of wool evenly in half and place behind the latch section of the hook, holding the two ends firmly together.

3 **Fastening the knot** Put the two ends of wool into the eye of the hook and pull the hook back through the loop, giving it a flick upwards as you do so.

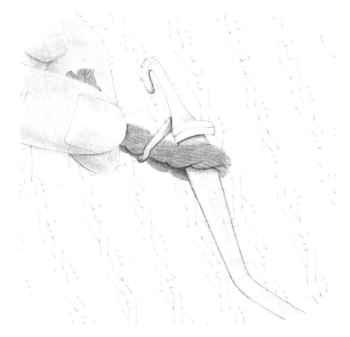

2 **Fitting in the canvas** Push the hook down through one square of canvas and up through the one immediately in front.

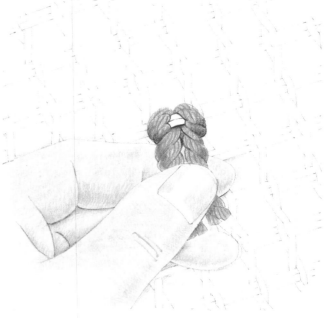

4 **Tightening the knot** Holding both ends of the wool firmly together, pull lightly on the two ends of the yarn to tighten the knot.

KEY

◻ white	◻ light orange	◼ bright pink	◼ light green
◼ dark purple	◼ bright purple	◻ medium pink	◼ dark green
◼ dark orange	◼ dark red	◻ light pink	

Shell picture frame

Beachcombing along a sandy bay is a great way to wile away a sunny afternoon during a holiday. You can find all kinds of treasures along the tide-line which can be collected and used later to decorate your home.

Here, we have used shells and rope to decorate a picture frame. It's a quick and easy way to create a unique holiday momento, and at the same time convert an old or plain picture frame into a more unusual ornament. If you frame up a holiday photo you will have an ideal gift for a favourite friend or granny. Add a

mirror and you will have a nautical accessory for your bathroom.

To copy our design choose a wide wooden frame with a textured finish; this will provide an interesting background as well as space for the rope and shells. If you can't find a frame with the appropriate finish try painting an existing frame yourself to give it a suitably distressed look.

Simply rub the frame surface with coarse glasspaper to remove any varnish and create a texture, then apply a coat of natural coloured matt emulsion paint.

▲ Golden oldies
A happy holiday snap of a day out becomes even more precious if you decorate the photo's frame with momentos gathered on the same day. Here, a wooden frame has been decorated with collected shells and rope and used to frame a treasured photo of children enjoying a day at the seaside. You can use the same technique to decorate a frame with dried flowers as a momento of a day in the country.

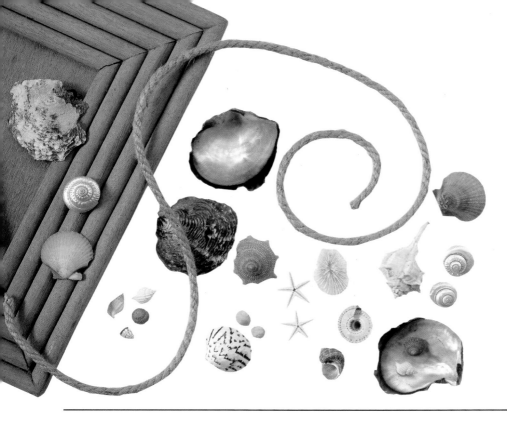

DECORATING THE FRAME

Materials
Wide wooden picture frame
Shells: Four pearl oyster shell halves roughly the same size, an assortment of **smaller shells** and **star fish** all in various colours, shapes and sizes
Jute rope 7mm thick and 2½m (3yds) long
Strong glue 2 tubes
Sharp scissors
Pins
Pencil and **white paper**

1 Arrange the shells Lay the frame out flat on a protected work surface. Place a pearl oyster shell on each corner with the curved edge facing outwards. Arrange smaller shells around and on top of these corner shells. Draw a quick pencil sketch to record the positions and colour of each shell.

2 Twist and twirl the rope Beginning at a corner, tuck one end of the rope under a large oyster shell. Twist and twirl the rope between, around, under and over the shells, knotting the rope and positioning the knots as desired. Pin the rope to the frame at close intervals to keep it in place. Check the design then update you sketch.

3 Secure the small shells Remove the oyster shells and any other shells that cover the rope and put them all to one side. Then working on the remaining shells, lift them off the frame one at a time and apply a small dab of glue to the underside and a line of glue along its edge, if needed. Then following the sketch, place it back on to the frame and hold it in place until the glue dries. Stick the smaller shells on the large oyster shells following the same technique. Test the shells have stuck.

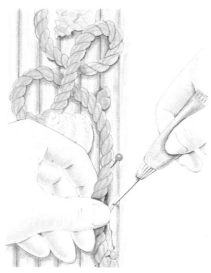

4 Glue the rope Remove a few pins from the rope, keeping the rest in position. Lift the loose section of rope away from the frame, and apply a line of glue to the frame under the rope. Press the section of the rope back down and hold in place for a few seconds until stuck. Stick all the rope in place in the same way, working a small section at a time. Leave glue to dry then remove pins.

5 Fix the remaining shells Following your pencil sketch, lay one large oyster shell in its correct position. Where the underneath of the shell touches the frame, rope or another shell, apply glue to these places. Firmly hold the shell in position until it is securely stuck. Apply the remaining large shells. Leave the frame flat for at least 10 minutes for the glue to bond.

6 Check security Check everything has been stuck in place, by gently trying to lift the shells and the rope, a section at a time. If there is any movement, lift away from the frame, apply more glue and hold in place until properly bonded in position. Gently stand the frame up and check once more that everything in stuck securely in place before framing your picture.

Fabric roses

A cluster of fabric roses surrounded by delicately stitched leaves is a delightful way to enhance your soft furnishings, and makes a charming alternative to the more traditional rosettes. You can use the roses to add softness and style to a tailored curtain tieback, or to embellish a pelmet, or swag and tail arrangement.

The roses look most effective teamed with an all-over floral print. Depending on your main fabric, either use only one colour to make up the cluster of roses, or select two or even three colours for a really striking effect.

The fabric used to make the roses should be stiff enough for them to hold their shape, but with enough flexibility

▲ Coming up roses
Soften the tailored outline of a classic tieback by adding a cluster of velvet roses in toning shades.

to be easily manageable and to form soft folds. Curtain velvet has an ideal texture for making fabric roses and will give the flowers depth and a soft outline.

TO MAKE THE ROSES

1 Cutting out Cut strips 70cm (27½in) long and 10cm (4in) wide from the fabric, cutting on the cross; cut one strip per rose, drawing up and cutting out the strips as shown to keep wastage to a minimum.

2 Trimming the strip Fold the strip in half lengthways and use tailor's chalk to mark curved ends on the strip; trim the ends into a curve, so that the rose will have a neat finish at its centre and outer edges.

Materials
Curtain velvet for the roses in the chosen shade(s) – a piece 120 × 50cm (47¼ × 19¾in) will be sufficient for seven roses and four or five rosebuds; for the leaves, use green furnishing velvet – a piece 50 × 25cm (19¾ × 10in) will make several leaves

Lightweight wadding 25 × 25cm (10 × 10in) for the leaves

Felt in a shade to match the roses, to cover their raw base

Buttonhole thread to gather the fabric; alternatively, use double sewing thread

Sewing thread in green or in a toning shade to stitch round the leaves

Sharp scissors

Long ruler

Tailor's chalk

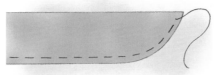

3 Stitching the strip Use a long running stitch and buttonhole thread to sew the two bottom edges of the strip together, with the stitches 6mm (¼in) in from the edge; follow the curves at both ends, and leave the gathering thread end loose.

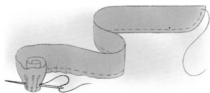

4 Gathering up the strip Pull the loose thread at one end of the strip to slightly gather the fabric at the opposite end. Starting at the loosely gathered end, begin rolling up the strip to form the centre of the rose; with a needle and a fresh length of sewing thread, secure the rolled up centre with a couple of stitches through its base.

5 Forming the rose Continue to roll up the fabric strip and stitch the rose; only gather the fabric very slightly at the start, as the centre of the rose is tightly rolled, then as you work the petals of the outer layers, gather the fabric more to make them splay out. Once the fabric strip is fully rolled up, secure the curved outer end with a few more stab stitches. Then secure and cut off the gathering thread.

TO MAKE THE ROSEBUDS

1 Cutting out Cut out strips of fabric 32cm (12½in) long and 8cm (3¼in) wide, cutting on the cross; the leftover fabric from making the roses will be sufficient for four or five rosebuds. Fold the strip, trim both ends and run a gathering stitch along the bottom edge, as for a rose.

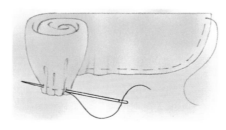

2 Forming the rosebud Roll up the centre of the bud very tightly, hardly gathering the fabric at all and not allowing the petals to splay out; secure with a few stab stitches through the base. As you roll up the strip, pull slightly on the gathering thread to help compress the fabric at the base of the bud, but keep the petals tightly packed. Towards the end of the strip, gather the fabric slightly more and allow the outer petals to spread out a little. Secure the bud and loose threads as usual.

TO MAKE THE LEAVES

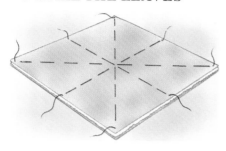

1 Preparing the fabric Cut the rectangle of fabric in half to give two equal squares. Sandwich the wadding between the two layers of fabric, with the edges lined up and the right sides of the fabric pieces facing outwards. Pin and tack the layers together.

2 Drawing the leaves With tailor's chalk, draw leaves on the fabric-wadding sandwich, using real rose leaves as a guide; make them 7cm (2¾in) long, and draw a central vein.

3 Zigzag stitching Zigzag stitch is used to stitch around the edges of the leaves and along the main vein. Set the machine stitch length to just past 0, and the stitch width to 4-5; you may need to slacken the top tension a little so that the interlock lies on the underside of the leaf. Practise on unused areas of the padded fabric until you get an even stitch with the threads lying close together. If working by hand, use satin stitch.

4 Stitching the leaves Starting at the base of the leaf, stitch along one side. As you approach the fine leaf tip, alter the stitch width to a narrower setting so it gives a finer outline. Reset the stitch width to its original size when you have stitched around the tip and are stitching down to the base. Stitch the vein in the same way, narrowing the tip to form a fine point. Snip off the threads close to the fabric. Repeat for all the leaves.

5 Cutting out the leaves Use a pair of sharp scissors to cut around the leaves, taking care not to catch the thread. Rub around the edges to loosen any fibres before the final trim.

▼ Roses galore
Velvet roses can be made in any colour of your choice, but nature's own shades are by far the most effective.

GROUPING THE FLOWERS

1 Arranging the flowers Make up as many roses, rosebuds and leaves as you require, then group them in an attractive arrangement, holding them against the article on which they are to be placed, such as a tieback, to judge the best effect. Bunch the roses up to form a fairly tight group and place the leaves around the outside, pinning them to hold them in place; try to make the grouping look random for a realistic effect. Stand back and check that you are happy with the overall effect.

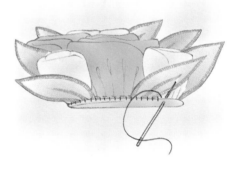

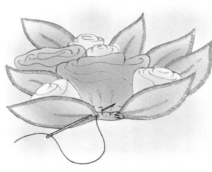

2 Stitching the flowers Once you are happy with the arrangement, stitch the roses, buds and leaves together, stitching through the bases of the flowers and securing the lower tips of the leaves just under the flower bases so that they splay out.

3 Covering the base Cut a square of felt large enough to fit over the raw base of the flower arrangement. Cover the base with a thin layer of rubber solution glue, then stick the felt over the base. Use scissors to trim the felt to within 6mm (¼in) of the base edge. Slip-stitch the felt to the lower sides of the flower arrangement, just above the raw edges of the base. Finally, slip-stitch the arrangement in place on to a tieback, or other article.

Satin Roses

Smaller, more delicate roses and leaves can be made from lengths of satin ribbon, and are a wonderful way to add freshness and style to cushions, bedspreads, bedheads and even the gathered-up sides of tablecloths; they are also ideal for sheer or lace curtain tiebacks, on which velvet roses would look too heavy.

Materials

Pink, red or ivory double-sided satin ribbon for the roses, 60-90cm (23½-35½in) long and 2.5-5cm (1-2in) wide.
Pale green single-sided satin ribbon for the leaves, 4cm (1½in) wide; 60cm (23½in) is sufficient for several leaves
Strip of lightweight wadding for leaves, 4cm (1½in) wide and 60cm (23½in) long
Sewing threads in matching shades
Non-fraying fabric for rose base; 50cm (19¾in) is sufficient
Sharp scissors and **tailor's chalk**

MAKING SATIN ROSES

1 Preparing the ribbon For the base, cut out a small square from the non-fraying fabric, about 10cm (4in) across. Take the length of ribbon and turn in 6mm (¼in) at one end to neaten the raw edge, then fold the ribbon in half lengthways.

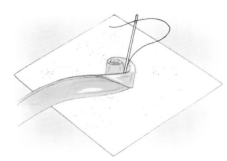

2 Rolling up the ribbon Centre the turned-in end of the ribbon on the fabric square and secure it with stab stitches through the base. Roll up a little of the ribbon to form a small, tight cone (the central petals of the rose), with the folded edge of the ribbon lying at the top of the rose; secure with stab stitches.

3 Forming the rose Wrap the ribbon around the rose centre in progressively looser loops, twisting the ribbon as you go, so that the folded edge lies first at the top and then at the base of the rose; secure the ribbon with tiny stab stitches at each twist, always finishing with the thread underneath the base fabric, and angling the stitches towards the centre of the rose as you move towards its outer edges.

4 Finishing the rose Once the rose is the desired size, cut off the end of the ribbon, allowing for an extra 6mm (¼in) to be turned in for a neat finish. Stitch the turned in end to the fabric base with stab stitches. Trim the edges of the base to just within the outer edge of the rose.

5 Making the leaves The leaves are made exactly as for the velvet roses, and their tips are stitched to the fabric base as previously described.

▲ **Floral appliqué**
Satin roses and leaves are easily stitched on to a fabric background; either attach them singly or in clusters, or as part of an appliqué design, varying the shade of the ribbon and also its width to make both small and large roses.

tip

Using fine fabrics

If you wish to make roses from a fine fabric, such as silk, it is possible to achieve the full, chunky look of the velvet roses with the aid of a little wadding. Simply cut a strip of lightweight wadding the same length as your fabric strip, and approximately half its width. Then sandwich it between the two layers of fabric when you fold the fabric strip in half. Stitch the gathering thread through both fabric and wadding, then make up the rose as usual.

Ribbon rose cushions

By cleverly folding and stitching lengths of ribbon you can produce lovely rose-shaped flowers and rose-buds. Then by combining these flowers with ribbon leaves and embroidered stems you can create these delightful pastel cushions.

The size and shape of the flowers will depend on the ribbon width and the length used. Here the larger flowers are made from 4cm (1½in) wide soft ribbon, the smaller ones from 25mm (1in) wide ribbon. These flowers have been made from double-sided matt ribbon which must be the same on both sides.

The simple shaped leaves are also cut from ribbon and edged-stitched with a closely-worked machine zigzag.

Once the flowers, buds and leaves have been created, you can sew them on to a shop-bought cushion or make up a cushion cover.

▼ Bouquet of roses
These ribbon roses are brought together with embroidered stems, to make a charming arrangement.

MAKING THE CREAM CUSHION

Materials

Cream moiré fabric 80 x 40cm (32 x 16in) plus bias strip for covering piping cord
Double-sided matt ribbon 4cm (1½in) wide: cream 1m (40in), pink 1m (40in), pale green 50cm (20in)
Double-sided matt ribbon 25mm (1in) wide: pink 65cm (26in), cream 15cm (6in), plus 28cm (11in) for the bow
White cotton oddment as backing
Matching sewing threads
Stranded embroidery cotton to match leaf ribbon
Piping cord 1.80m (2yd) length
Cushion pad 37cm (14½in) square

1 Cut the cover pieces From moiré fabric cut two 40cm (16in) squares for the cushion cover.

2 Beginning the large roses Make one pink and one cream flower in the same way. Cut a 6cm (2¼in) square of white cotton fabric. Using the 1m (40in) length of 40mm (1½in) wide ribbon, pin one end on to the white cotton and fold a pentagon, with sides 7cm (26¾in) long.

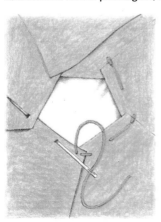

3 Adding more petals Stitch through the backing fabric at each inner corner as shown, to hold the ribbon in place. Continue tacking the ribbon round the base, folding another slightly smaller pentagon on top of the first one, but positioning the folded points of this round to the middle of previous sides, forming the rose.

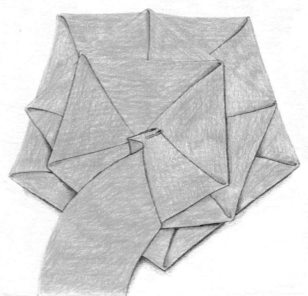

4 Filling the centre Fold round another slightly smaller circle on top of the two previous rounds with points in the centre of previous row.

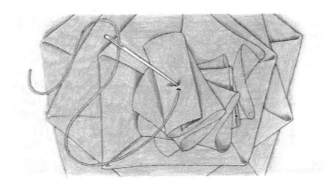

5 Completing the rose Stitch down the centre of the last 20cm (8in) of the ribbon, using large stitches to gather and twist the ribbon, tuck the raw edge under at the very end. Stitch in place. Press each rose flat.

6 Making a small rose
Make one smaller pink flower to complete the arrangement. Cut a 3cm (1¼in) square of backing fabric. Cut a 50cm (20in) length of 25mm (1in) wide ribbon, and make up the small rose in the same way as the large roses, with three rounds of folded petals and a gathered centre made from the remaining 12cm (5in) of ribbon. Fold each side so it is approximately 5cm (2in) long. Press the completed flower flat under a cloth.

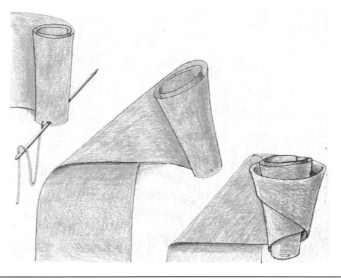

7 Creating a rosebud
Make two rosebuds one from cream ribbon and one from pink ribbon. Cut a 15cm (6in) length of 25mm (1in) wide ribbon. Wind up tightly from one end for three rounds and catch at the base with a few stitches. Fold the ribbon end diagonally away from the bud and turn the bud on to the fold centring it; repeat, then fasten with a few stitches at the base. To neaten, fasten the ribbon end at the back, to form the bud.

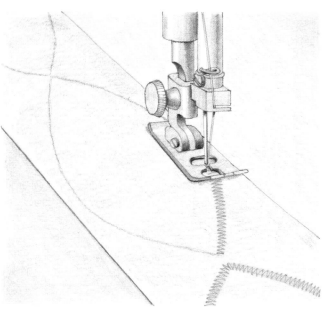

8 Making the leaves
Trace off both leaf patterns on to firm tracing paper and cut them out. Draw round large leaf pattern five times on 40mm (1½in) wide pale green ribbon. Zigzag stitch round each leaf, following the marked outline. If working by hand, use satin stitch. Use a pair of sharp scissors to cut around the leaves. Make up three smaller leaves using the same method. To vary the foliage choose another, darker shade of green ribbon.

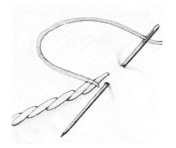

9 Embroidering stems
Following the diagram overleaf, gently mark the stem positions across the front cover. Using three strands of embroidery cotton, work stem stitch along each marked line. Below the bow position, increase the width of the stem stitches.

10 Arranging flowers
Pin the ribbon roses, leaves and rosebuds over the cushion front, following the diagram and covering over the embroidered stems. Carefully catch stitch each flower, leaf and rosebud in place with invisible stitches. Carefully match the thread to the colour of the cushion, so the stitches will disappear.

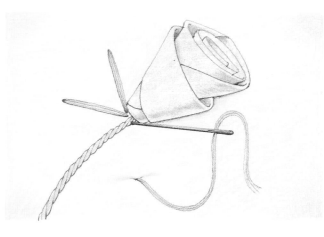

11 Embroidering calyx
Using three strands of green embroidery cotton, work four large stem stitch fanning out from the base of each rosebud to form the calyx of the flower following the diagram. Make all four lines the same length but not too long. Also embroider a few stitches on to the bud to join the calyx to it.

12 Adding the bow Cut a 28cm (11in) length of ribbon; choose either the pink ribbon or the cream ribbon. Tie the ribbon into a bow. Trim ribbon ends into Vs, to prevent fraying. Catch stitch the bow over base of stems, as shown in the diagram overleaf.

13 Making up the piping cord
Cover piping cord with bias fabric strip. With cord facing inwards and raw edges matching together, pin and stitch piping cord round front cushion 1.5cm (⅝in) from the edges. Butt together at edges to finish off.

14 Assembling the cushion cover
Place back cover to front with right sides together; pin and stitch together all round leaving an 30cm (12in) opening centrally in base edge. Trim seams and corners and turn cover right side out. Insert pad and slipstich close.

33

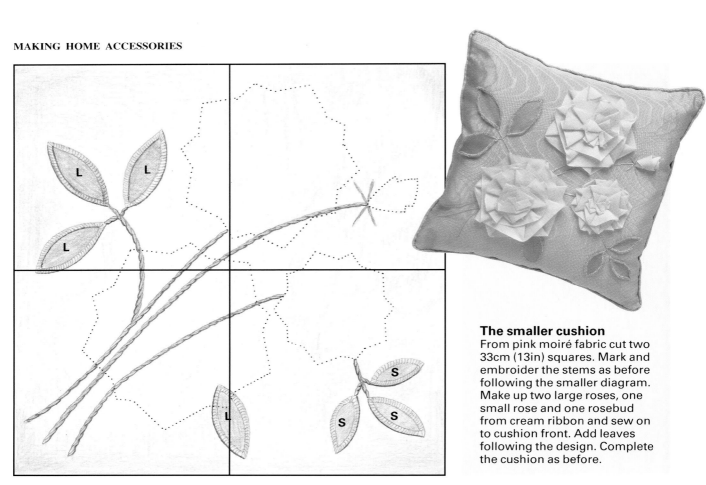

The smaller cushion
From pink moiré fabric cut two 33cm (13in) squares. Mark and embroider the stems as before following the smaller diagram. Make up two large roses, one small rose and one rosebud from cream ribbon and sew on to cushion front. Add leaves following the design. Complete the cushion as before.

▲ *Small pink cushion*
This is the design for the smaller cushion. Embroider the stems then arrange the leaves. The roses cover the parts shown by dotted lines.

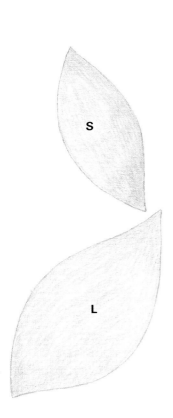

◀ *Patterns for leaves*
Trace off the actual-size patterns for the leaves.

▲ *Large cushion* Once the stems have been embroidered, place the roses and buds in position following the dotted lines. Stitch the bow on last.

A dough basket

▲ **Flowers forever** *This easy to make dough basket, which hangs on the wall, is the perfect framework for long-lasting displays of dried or silk flowers.*

This charming wall basket, overflowing with foliage and flowers is the perfect decoration for a country home. Made from salt dough and baked in the oven the basket makes the ideal framework for a long-lasting winter display, using either silk or dried material.

Salt dough is a surprisingly good modelling material. It's cheap and easily made from store cupboard ingredients and the high salt content, along with the glycerine, ensures the dough has a firm consistency which won't crumble. This basket is constructed over a mound of crumpled kitchen foil, using short lengths of dough, moulded and overlapped to create a traditional basket-weave pattern.

Decide on the location for your basket display and choose flowers and foliage to suit the room scheme. Then when necessary, you can re-arrange the display to suit the time of year. For example, here the purple flowers can be substituted by red berries for a festive Christmas display.

Materials

Plain superfine flour 240g (8oz)
Salt 180g (6oz)
Glycerine 2 tsp
Gloss varnish
Kitchen foil and **cling wrap**
Mixing bowls 20-23cm (8-9in) across for mould and larger one for mixing the dough
Pastry board, rolling pin and **baking tray**
Selection of silk or dried seed pods, berries and flowers
Florist's wire
Florist's foam, for dried flowers
Clear adhesive

MAKING A BASKET

1 Mixing the dough Mix the salt, flour and glycerine together in the large mixing bowl. Add some water, a little at a time and combine until the dough leaves the sides of the bowl and forms a ball. Knead the dough for several minutes until it is smooth and pliable. Cover with cling wrap.

2 Creating a mould Line the small mixing bowl with a sheet of foil, so it overlaps the rim. Scrunch up more foil and press firmly into half of the bowl until it reaches the top. Fold foil sheet around the crumpled pieces; remove from bowl.

3 Forming the back Place a portion of the dough on the pastry board. Roll it out to a 6mm (¼in) thickness. Place the mould flat side down on the dough and cut round, leaving a 1cm (⅜in) border all round. Place both on the baking tray.

4 Beginning the basket Mark a dotted line (**A**) down the centre of the foil mould, then one on either side 2.5cm (1in) apart (**B**). and (**C**). Roll a small piece of dough into a long sausage shape, 6mm (¼in) in diameter and 14cm (5½in) long. Lay this vertically along line (**A**). Roll out a similar shape and cut into 5cm (2in) strips. Lay these horizontally over the vertical strip between lines (**B**) and (**C**) leaving similar sized gaps in between.

5 Starting to weave Roll out another dough strip the same size as before and lay it vertically along line (**C**) covering the ends of the short horizontal strips. Then cut more short strips in the same way as before and lay them horizontally over line (**C**) in the gaps left in the previous row, creating a basket weave effect.

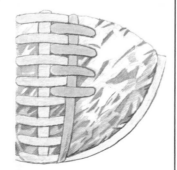

6 Dealing with edges Continue to work the dough strips across the right-hand side of the foil mould in the same way, graduating the pattern to fit around the mould until you reach the outside edge. Trim and stick the ends of each strip to the dough base with a little water.

7 Weaving the left side Starting with a long dough strip placed along line (**B**), repeat the same pattern across the basket in the opposite direction, so the pattern will match across the whole basket. Trim and stick the ends to the dough base with water.

8 Adding a handle Roll out two thicker sausage shaped strips 38cm (15in) long. Twist the two lengths together to form the basket handle. Lay on the baking tray and press ends into the inside of the basket.

9 Finishing off To neaten the top, roll out two 38cm (15in) long sausage shaped strips. Twist them together and lay over the top of the weaving. Trim ends to fit and stick to base. Roll two 7cm (2¾in) long sausage shaped strips and twist together to form the basket base. Stick to base trimming back carefully to fit.

10 Baking the dough basket Preheat the oven to 110°C/225°F/Gas Mark 2. Place the tray with the dough basket in the oven. Bake for 4-5 hours, or 3-4 hours for a fan-assisted oven. Check that the dough is baked hard. Remove from oven and leave to dry for 2-3 days. Carefully remove the foil, using tweezers.

11 Varnishing the basket When completely dry, paint with two coats of varnish, allowing the basket to dry between each coat.

12 Decorating the basket Cut and wedge the florist's foam to fit into the basket. Fill the basket with dried or silk flowers and foliage. Position the largest flowers and leaves first to form the basic framework of the arrangement, then fill in with the remaining material. If the flower or leaf stems are too short or brittle and break, use fine florist's wire and foam to secure the flowers and leaves into the foam. To create a cascading arrangement stick a few sprigs of foliage on to or through the basket-weave.

Cover story

Address books, diaries, and other volumes that contain information about the family and home often have uninspiring covers. They simply fade into the background when surrounded by the glossy covers of cookery books and coffee-table publications. So, for a chic, individual look, cover your diary, address book, birthday book or family photo albums with remnants of fabric, either especially selected for the task, or left over from the furnishings of a specific room for a perfect match.

You can have fun choosing fabrics to cover a co-ordinated set of books for a particular room, or make a set as a present for a friend, carefully selecting the fabrics to match their home.

▼ Co-ordinated look
Choosing co-ordinated fabrics to cover your diary and address book will make keeping your engagements an absolute delight.

Materials
Hardbacked address book or **diary**
Mediumweight fabric remnant to cover book with at least 5cm (2in) all round
Spray adhesive available from art shops
Sharp pointed fabric scissors
Old newspapers
Fabric glue
Spray fabric protector
Knitting needle
Satin ribbon for bookmark 6mm (¼in) wide and 10cm (4in) longer than spine

COVERING THE BOOK

1 Preparing the fabric Iron the fabric and select any motifs you wish to centre on the front cover, then trim fabric to within 5cm (2in) around book. Fold fabric in half to find the centre point to match the book spine, and snip into ends of fold. Then, working in a well ventilated area protected with newspaper, place fabric wrong side up on the newspaper and spray evenly with adhesive holding the can 15-20cm (6-8in) from the surface. Lay fabric flat, sticky side up on a clean work surface.

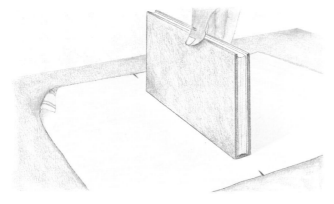

2 Position the book Leave for a few seconds until the adhesive is tacky, then line the snips in the fabric with the centre of the book spine both top and bottom and press the book down firmly on to the fabric.

3 Cover the book Smooth the fabric away from the spine over the back and front towards the edges. Check for air bubbles, peel off and reposition fabric if necessary. Trim the fabric to within 3cm (1¼in) all round.

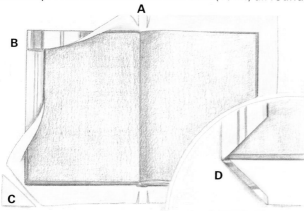

4 Neatening the edges Snip the fabric each side of the spine to within 5mm (¼in) of the book (A). Fold the fabric over the edges of the book to check the fit (B). Peel back the fabric around corners and trim excess fabric (C) then reposition with neater mitred corners (D).

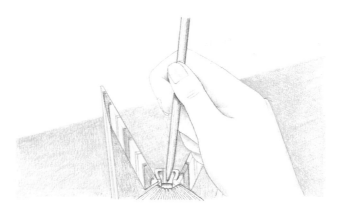

5 Neaten the book spine Trim the fabric each end of the spine to within 1.5cm (5/8in) of the book. Open book and with the covers pulled right back, fold the fabric over the edge, then use the knitting needle to push the fabric into the spine and smooth in place.

6 Finish covering the book Open the book and place newspaper under the fly leaf and over the inside front cover, then evenly spray the fly leaf with adhesive; remove the newspaper and carefully close the book. Open the book to check the fly leaf has been stuck securely in place and is covering the raw edges of fabric. Repeat for back cover.

7 Adding a book mark If your book requires a book mark, dab a spot of fabric glue on one end of the ribbon. Open the book and pushing the covers back to allow easy access, glue the ribbon to the paper spine. Leave glue to dry then trim end of ribbon at an angle.

8 Caring for the book Protecting the work surface with newspaper and following the manufacturers instructions, evenly spray the book cover with fabric protector.

Covering up
If your fabric is pale coloured you may find that the original book cover shows through. To prevent this, first cover the book with white paper.

▼ **All change**
Transform your books with fabric covers.

Coffee pot cosies

The traditional jug and cafetière coffee pots make really tasty coffee, but unfortunately they have no way of keeping the coffee hot, unless of course you use a cosy cover. These two cosies can be made to fit almost any size of coffee pot and will bring colour to your table as well.

Made from a tiny strawberry print fabric, borders on the main covers are decorated with larger strawberry motifs cut from spotted fabric to give the illusion of the tiny seeds. These are appliqued into place using machine satin stitch and topped with tiny, green ribbon caylix.

This cafetière cover is made with a padded base but no lid, to accommodate the plunger knob. The cover is held on to the pot with a matching ribbon bow.

The coffee pot cosy overleaf has a hexagonal shape and a cover for the lid. The centre panel at the front incorporates a decorative climbing strawberry plant cut from the same fabrics and trimmed with Russia braid. The side seams are left unstitched to accommodate the handle and spout.

▲ *Take a break*
The promise of a rich tasting cup of coffee during a mid-morning break or after dinner is all the more pleasing when you know the coffee will be piping hot and served with pretty matching china.

Both pot covers have an inner layer of wadding to provide the insulation around the pots. This cafetière pot is 18cm (7in) high with an 11cm (4½in) diameter the other coffee pot is 23cm (9in) high with a 15cm (6in) diameter.

COFFEE POT COVER

Materials

Printed fabric with tiny strawberry motif 90 x 25cm (36 x 10in)

Plain green fabric 36 x 20cm (14 x 8in)

Lightweight wadding 90 x 40cm (36 x 16in)

Russia braid in dark green 1.80m (2yd)

Plain cream fabric for lining 90 x 40cm (36 x 16in)

Red and white spotted fabric for strawberries 40 x 10cm (16 x 4in)

Paper for patterns

Sewing thread to match fabrics

Iron-on bonding web

1 Measuring the pot Make a paper pattern by measuring the pot. Measure the circumference at the widest part (omitting the spout and handle) and add 4cm (1½in) to allow for wadding (**A**); the circumference around the lid plus 4cm (1½in) (**B**); the height of the pot to the lid (**C**) and lid to the top of the knob (**D**).

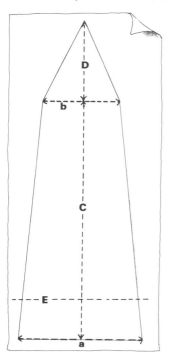

2 Making the pattern Divide the circumference measurement (**A**) by six and draw a horizontal line to this measurement (**a**) on a sheet of paper. Mark a vertical line equal to the height of the pot (measurements **C** plus **D**) in the centre of (**a**). Divide measurement (**B**) by six and mark a horizontal line to this measurement (**b**) between (**C**) and (**D**). Join up the lines to form the side panel pattern.

3 Cutting out wadding Add 1.5cm (⅝in) to the pattern piece all round for seam allowances. Using this pattern cut out six pieces in wadding and also six pieces in cream lining fabric.

4 Cutting out fabric Measure 4cm (1½in) up from the base edge of the panel pattern and cut across pattern line (**E**) for the border. Add 1.5cm (⅝in) seam allowance all round both pieces. Using the top piece cut six from patterned fabric. Using base pattern cut six pieces from plain green fabric for the bottom band.

▲ **Budding berries**
Afternoon coffee will never be the same again once you have your own strawberry coffee pot cover. It's almost a perfect excuse to treat yourself to strawberry tarts, just as a finishing touch! If you prefer a different type of fruit you could always alter the design.

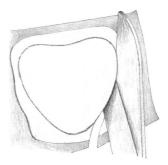

5 Making the motifs Trace off the small strawberry template. Mark round the outline on bonding web. Cut out roughly. Fuse the bonding web to the wrong side of the red fabric. Cut out. Repeat until you have twenty-four berries. Trace off the leaf template. Make up six leaf shapes in green fabric in the same way.

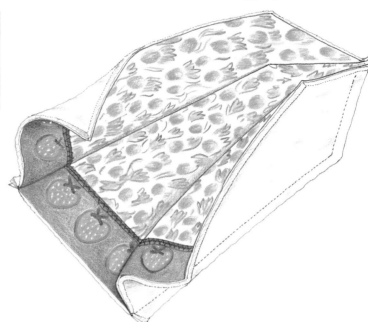

6 **Stitching strawberries in place** Iron to fuse three evenly spaced strawberries between seam allowance on one green base band. Work a tight satin stitch round the strawberries. Use green thread to stitch stalks. Repeat to add strawberries to all the green bands.

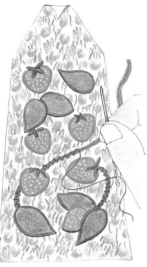

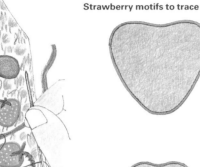

Strawberry motifs to trace

Leaf motif to trace

7 **Creating a panel** Fuse the remaining six berries and the leaves to one patterned panel as shown, overlapping the leaves and fruit. Satin stitch in place. Then stitch lengths of Russia braid between them as stems.

9 **Padding the cover** Pin a piece of wadding to the wrong side of each panel piece. Pin and stitch three panels together, to form half the cover. Trim the seams, cutting the wadding close to the stitching. Pin and stitch the remaining panels together with the appliqué panel in the centre of the three; trim seams as before. Zigzag stitch a length of Russia braid to the right side over the seamlines.

10 **Stitching the cover together** Place the two halves together; pin and stitch remaining seams, leaving an opening in both seams to accommodate the coffee pot handle and spout. Fasten off the seams on either side of openings with a few back stitches. Trim seams back.

11 **Adding the lining** Pin and stitch lining sections together, leaving the top sections of the two side seams unstitched. Place lining to main cover with right sides together, matching seamlines. Pin and stitch round the base edge. Trim seams and turn cover right side out, check fit on coffee pot.

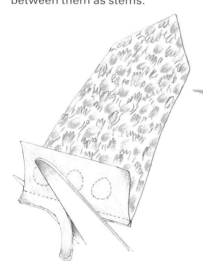

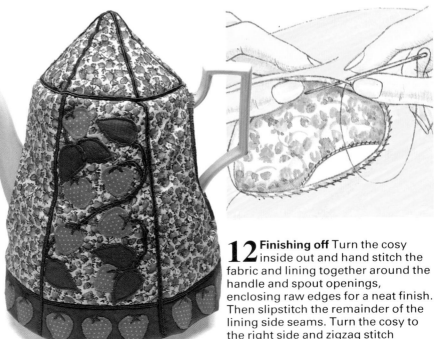

8 **Stitching on green bands** Pin and stitch one green base band to each patterned panel. Trim seam allowance. Zigzag stitch a length of Russia braid to the right side over each of the seamlines.

12 **Finishing off** Turn the cosy inside out and hand stitch the fabric and lining together around the handle and spout openings, enclosing raw edges for a neat finish. Then slipstitch the remainder of the lining side seams. Turn the cosy to the right side and zigzag stitch Russia braid around the top of the lid.

CAFETIERE COVER
Materials
Printed fabric with tiny strawberry motif 12 x 50cm (4¾ x 20in)
Green fabric 40 x 50cm (16 x 20in)
Cream fabric 10 x 50cm (4 x 20in)
Red and white spotted fabric 20 x 10cm (8 x 4in)
Lightweight wadding 50 x 30cm (20 x 12in)
Russia braid in green 2.50m (2¾yd)
Green ribbon 25mm x 70cm (1 x 28in)
Green ribbon 3mm x 60cm (⅛ x 24in)
Iron-on quilting interfacing 20 x 10cm (8 x 4in)
Sewing thread and **paper for patterns**

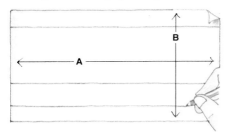

1 Making the pattern Measure the circumference of the cafetière (minus the handle) and add 3.5cm (1⅜in) for padding (**A**). Measure the height of the pot (**B**). On a sheet of paper, draw a rectangle to this size. Adding 1.5cm (⅝in) seam allowance cut one piece in wadding and one in green fabric.

2 Cutting fabric bands Divide the pattern horizontally into four bands. Cut along the lines. Adding 1.5cm (⅝in) seam allowance all round cut out the four strips. the top and base bands in green, a narrow cream band and a wide patterned band.

3 Making up the strawberries Trace off the large strawberry motif. Mark the outline on to interfacing. Cut out interfacing roughly and fuse on to the wrong side of red and white spotted fabric. Cut out round the outline. Repeat to cut twelve strawberries in the same way.

4 Stitching strawberries in place Evenly space strawberries along the cream band. Iron in place. Stitch all round each strawberry with a close satin stitch. Cut a 7.5cm (3in) length of narrow ribbon. Fold into three loops and hand stitch to the top of each strawberry.

5 Sewing the bands Sew the coloured bands together in the order shown to make up the cover.

▼ *Made to measure*
Almost any coffee pot can have a made to measure cosy to keep its liquid contents hot. You could even design your own pot cover, but remember to buy machine washable fabrics.

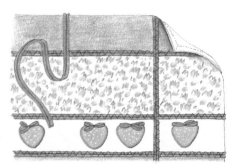

6 Stitching wadding Pin wadding to the wrong side of the fabric panel. Zigzag stitch a length of Russia braid to the right side over each seamline and vertically to outline panels. Ensure the braid does not cover any strawberries.

7 Making a base Draw around the cafetière base to make a pattern and add 1.5cm (⅝in) all round. Cut two bases from green fabric and one from wadding. Pin wadding to wrong side of one fabric base, then stitch panel to base. Stitch up back seam for 2cm (¾in).

8 Adding a lining With right sides facing back edge pin and stitch lining and base together as for corner. Place lining to cover, and stitch top edge. Turn.

9 Making ribbon ties Cut wider ribbon in half widthways. Pin each length into top of back opening. Slipstitch lining to main fabric down back opening, catching in ribbon. Trim ribbon ends diagonally.

Decorating trays

A simple wooden tray can be quickly transformed into a stylish show-piece with a sheet of gift-wrap paper and some paint. This idea is a great way to smarten-up a less-than-perfect tray, giving it a new lease of life. Based on the centuries-old craft of découpage, the chosen motifs are carefully cut from gift-wrap paper and pasted into the painted tray base.

There is a huge range of gift-wrap paper available, but the motifs for this project must be chosen with care. The paper must be sufficiently thick to withstand a coat of wallpaper paste, the

outlines must be easy to define and each motif should be effective enough to stand as a single pattern. Different papers can be mixed and matched, especially if you want to keep within a particular colour range or favourite flower. Border designs can be used to outline a central theme or abstract figures could be haphazardly placed for a modern interpretation.

Paint the base of the tray with a strong deep colour that will contrast and highlight the design. Then highlight the side walls of the tray, by picking out one of the motif's colours and paint the edges

▲ Floral tray
A glorious arrangement of stylized flowers, leaves and butterflies decorate the base of this tray. The delicate colours of the flowers harmonize together, while at the same time contrasting against the strongly coloured background. The tray edges are picked out in gold.

to give the tray an extra touch of class. Finally seal the design under several coats of varnish to make the tray serviceable as well as a delight to view when stored in the kitchen.

43

DECORATING YOUR TRAY

Materials

Wooden tray with square upper edge
Fine glasspaper
Paintbrushes
Dark undercoat and **black or similar dark coloured emulsion paint** for background
Gold paint
Removable low-tack masking tape
Gift-wrap paper with strong motif
Wallpaper paste
Satin-finish acrylic varnish
Small sharp paper scissors

1 Undercoating the tray If the tray is second hand, check it over for flaws and clean well. Apply one coat of dark-coloured undercoat paint over all surfaces including the base and allow to dry.

2 Painting the tray Apply two coats of emulsion paint over the undercoat for the background. Allow to dry. Rub down between each coat.

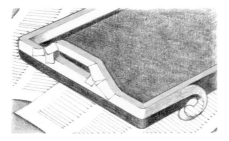

3 Adding the gold edges Mask along either side of the tray edges with tape, smooth down the edges, to provide a good barrier. Carefully paint the gold between the masking strips and leave to dry. When dry, carefully peel off the masking tape.

4 Cutting out the paper motifs Choose the motifs from the gift-wrap paper. Carefully cut out the chosen motifs from the paper. Work with a continuous cutting action to gain a smooth outline. Arrange motifs over the tray base.

5 Fixing the motifs Mix up the wallpaper paste. Coat the back of each motif and stick in place. Check that all edges are well stuck down. Gently smooth over each piece with a soft cloth and allow to dry. Overlap some motifs to complete the design.

6 Varnishing the completed design Apply three coats of acrylic varnish over the design until it is well sealed and you have a tough durable finish. Allow plenty of drying time between coats of varnish. Rub down between coats with glasspaper.

 tip

Easy decoration

If time is at a premium, you can simply paint the tray then decorate it with a sheet of pretty gift-wrap. Cut the paper to size and paste it on to the base. Seal the tray with three coats of varnish as before to make it stain resistant.

Seasonal tie-backs

Bring the countryside into your home and hold back your curtains with natural looking tie-backs. These pretty but practical curtain accessories have been made from lengths of rope and decorated with shells for use during the summer months, while another set, for the winter, is trimmed with seasonal silk foliage, nuts and pine cones.

The tie-backs look particularly good against creamy coloured curtains either in a conservatory or at French windows leading on to a balcony or garden.

Sea shells look exquisite against the natural jute rope. Pick up large shells from the beach to make a tie-back with holiday memories, or use the more exotic types of shells which are available from specialist shops.

For the winter, cheer up a gloomy outlook by trimming the tie-backs with richly coloured seasonal foliage made of silk. This can look very realistic and has the advantage of never drying out.

◄ Sea view
Compliment the naïve seashells with large sea blue glass beads threaded on to rope for a nautical theme.

Materials
Manila rope 20mm (¾in) thick, 3 lengths each 70cm (27½in) long
Jute natural garden twine 1 ball
PVA adhesive
Sharp scissors
Adhesive tape
Tape measure
Tapestry needle
Decorations selection of shells and blue glass beads or silk foliage
Strong glue
White piping cord 6m (6⅝yd)

SHELL TIE-BACK

If you only decorate the front half of each tie-back, make sure that you create a pair for a set of curtains.

1 Preparing the rope Bind the ends of the rope with adhesive tape to prevent it unravelling.

2 Attaching twine loops Untwist one end of one rope to provide a gap between the three strands. Thread a 70cm (27½in) length of garden twine through the rope 4cm (1½in) from the end. Take the twine round one strand and back through the top to where it was first inserted leaving an end 16cm (6¼in) long; knot ends securely. Attach a length of twine to the rope's ends.

3 Making hanging loops Place rope lengths side by side. Keeping the ends level, plait the three long ends of twine for 28cm (11in). Securely knot plait ends and short twine ends together at plait end to make a loop. Trim twine ends. Make a hanging loop in the same way at the other end.

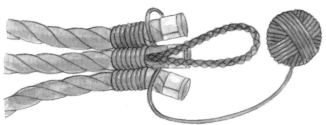

4 Neatening the rope ends Remove the adhesive tape. Tie one end of the twine to the hanging loop knot. Holding the hanging loop flat against the back of the middle rope, use the twine to weave around the three rope ends sewing them together covering all the knots to within 2cm (¾in) of ends. Apply adhesive over the last 2cm (¾in) of rope. Continue weaving until all the ends have been covered. Finish by taking the twine under the woven end, then wrapping it tightly between the ropes, knot twine securely at the back to finish.

5 Positioning the decorations Fold the tie-back in half, bringing the hanging loops together to find the centre point and mark with a pin. Only the side of the tie-back that shows at the front will need to be decorated. Lay tie-back flat on your work surface. Arrange the decorations on a flat surface to give you some idea of their order along the rope. Decide which beads will hang below the rope.

6 Attaching the decorations Use strong glue to stick the shells in place on to the tie-back. Wind the piping cord three times round the end of the tie-back catching in the end. Then wind the cord round the tie-back looping round the shells and knotting on glass beads at intervals across the base edge. Take the cord to the opposite end of the tie-back and wind round the end in the same way. Trim off ends.

FLOWER TIE-BACK

Seasonal foliage can also be used to decorate the basic rope tie-back. Choose silk leaves and combine them with hips and berries, hazlenuts and fir cones. Use strong glue to stick the nuts in place and slot the stalks of the remaining pieces into natural and green twine wound round and round the rope.

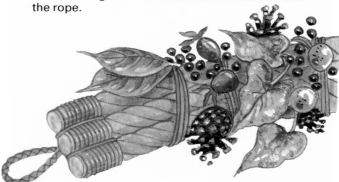

Wind twine in natural and green round and round the rope to provide a mesh in which to stick the foliage; knot the ends firmly on to the rope. Make a stalk for the fir cones by winding a length of wire round the base of the cone and then twisting the ends to form a stalk.

Lace-framed pot pourri

Preserving the scent of summer flowers to enjoy throughout the year is a tradition that has been around for generations. There are a variety of ways to display pot pourri but maybe one of the prettiest is to frame it in lace between two layers of tulle or fine net. You can then hang it on the wall in a bathroom or bedroom so that every time you enter you will catch its fragrance. Framing pot pourri like this, using a flexi-hoop is so quick and easy that it will take next to no time to make several more as gifts for family and friends. Vary the colours of the materials to suit the surrounding decor and fill with flower mixes other than the pot pourri, such as lavender, roses or fragrant herbs like camomile or thyme.

▼ Scented ideas
A lovely way to present pot pourri is to frame it in lace and allow the scent to waft throughout the room.

Materials

Flexi-hoop with woodgrain finish 10cm (4in) diameter

Lightweight cotton fabric to cover backing card 14 x 28cm (5½ × 11in)

Tulle or fine net fabric 25 × 50cm (10 × 19¾in)

Thin card 12cm (4¾in) square

Pencil

Scissors

Glue stick

Pot pourri either home-made or shop bought

Sewing thread to match tulle

Needle size 3

Lace to match tulle 2cm (¾in) wide × 60cm (23½in) long

Purchased ribbon roses × 3

Narrow ribbon 2mm (⅛in) wide, 30cm (12in) for hanging and 150cm (60in) for the bow.

MAKING THE SCENTED FRAME

1 Cutting the card Place the inner half of the flexi-hoop on to the card and draw around the inside of the frame. Cut out the circle.

2 Cutting the cotton fabric Using the card circle as a template, draw two circles on to the fabric. Cut out one circle following the drawn line and the second 1cm (⅜in) larger than the line all round.

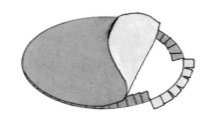

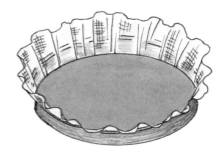

3 Covering the card backing Lay the larger fabric circle right side down on the work surface. Apply a little glue to one side of the card circle and stick it to the centre. Turn the work over and smooth out any air bubbles before snipping the fabric into the edge of the card. Apply a line of glue around the card edge, fold over the snipped sections and stick in place. Neaten by gluing the second fabric circle in place on top.

4 Backing the frame Cut two pieces of tulle 5cm (2in) larger all round than the outer half of the flexi-hoop. Place the inner half of the hoop on the work surface and lay one piece of tulle over it. Push the backing card into the frame, best side down, so that it is flat on the work surface.

5 Filling with pot pourri Smear glue over the fabric surface facing upwards, then fill the hoop with colourful pot pourri to the top edge of the frame.

6 Securing the cover Lay the second tulle circle over the pot pourri and adjusting the top piece of tulle to keep it taut, clip the outer part of the flexi-hoop in place and trim tulle edge close to the frame.

7 Adding the lace Using small running stitches, gather up the lace to fit around the frame, then carefully stitch to the tulle edge at the back of the frame.

8 Attaching the hanging ribbon Thread the ribbon through the hanging loop and knot the ends together securely.

9 Adding the trim Cut the remaining ribbon into 3 equal lengths, knot these lengths together at the centre and tie to form a bow. Stitch bow in place at the bottom of the frame and finish by sewing the ribbon roses in place.

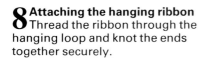

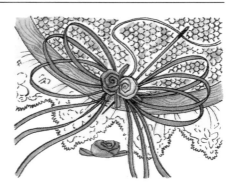

Table-top tidies

Fabric-covered containers, like the tray and notelet holder shown here, make smart accessories for desktops and dressing-tables, and will keep clutter at bay. By using the same fabrics to cover two or three items, you can create a co-ordinated set in the colours and patterns of your choice.

All of the items featured here are made up from pieces of stiff card, covered with fabric, and stitched or glued into shape; each one is then trimmed with matching ribbon to add the final decorative touch. Use two or more co-ordinated fabrics, and base your choice on what the set is to be used for, as well as on your own personal preference; for example, floral fabrics in soft shades will make a charming dressing-table set in a bedroom, while stronger colours and a simple design will be ideal for a desk set in the study. Use a

▲ Striking combinations
The key to creating stunning table-top sets lies in a stylish choice of fabrics, like this classical combination of maroon and navy.

firmly woven fabric which will fully conceal the card underneath, and match the colours and design of other soft furnishings in the room.

Materials
Stiff card to make up the containers
Fabric plus contrast fabric for lining. (See instructions for quantities.)
Satin ribbon 15mm (⅝in) wide to match the fabrics; you will need 3m (3½yds)
Matching sewing threads
Rubber solution adhesive

DRESSING-TABLE TRAY

The tray is made up from a flat piece of card, with the corners drawn up and tied in place with ribbon bows.

1 Cutting out From stiff card, cut a rectangle measuring 30.5 x 20cm (12 x 8in), two strips 30.5 x 4cm (12 x 1½in), and another two 20 x 4cm (8 x 1½in). Cut two fabric rectangles (one from contrast fabric) measuring 41.5 x 31cm (16½ x 12½in). Trim a 4.5cm (1¾in) square from each corner of the fabric rectangles.

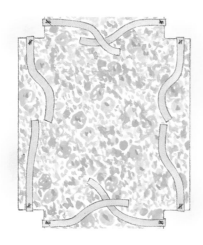

2 Attaching the ribbons Cut eight 18cm (7in) lengths of ribbon. Lay out main fabric piece, right side up. Tack one end of a ribbon length to one of the outer corners of fabric piece, matching ribbon's raw end to inside edge of corner, but placing its side 1cm (½in) in from the side of the fabric rectangle. Tack other seven ribbons in place at the corners.

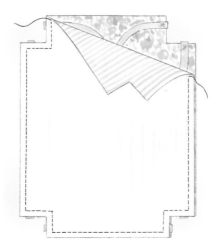

3 Stitching the tray With right sides together and edges matching, place the second fabric piece over the first, making sure all the ribbon ends are tucked in. Taking a 1cm (½in) seam allowance, pin and stitch around the edges of the fabric, leaving one short end open. Remove tacking stitches from ribbons. Snip into seam allowances at corners, turn through to right side and press.

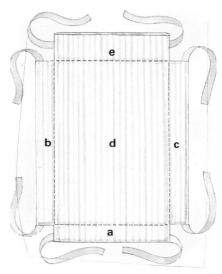

4 Inserting the cards Slip one of the short, narrow card strips (**a**) between the two layers of fabric, to lie opposite the unstitched opening; push it right up against the outer seam, then machine stitch next to it, through both layers of fabric using a zip foot. Insert and stitch in place first one and then the other long side strips of card (**b** and **c**), followed by the central rectangle (**d**), and finally the strip next to the opening (**e**). Fold in the open edges and slipstitch or glue closed.

5 Forming the tray Snip the ends of the ribbons to shape them into a decorative point. Tie each pair of ribbons at the corners into full bows, lifting the sides of the rectangle together to form a tray.

DRESSING-TABLE POT

Like the tray, the pot is made up from individual rectangles of card, held together by their fabric cover, but its base is covered separately, then glued or stitched in place. A ribbon trim gives the pot a decorative finish.

1 Cutting out From stiff card, cut four rectangles measuring 11 x 8cm (4 x 3in), and one 8cm (3in) square. From your fabric, cut two rectangles (one in the contrast lining fabric) measuring 35.5 x 13cm (13¾ 4 x 5in), together with two 9cm (3½in) squares (one in contrast fabric).

2 Stitching the cover With right sides together and edges matching, stitch the two fabric rectangles together, down both short sides and along one long edge, taking a 1cm (½in) seam allowance. Trim seam allowances, turn through to right side and press.

▼ Flowers and stripes
Two differently patterned fabrics in co-ordinating shades, like the green stripe and floral print of this dressing-table set, can make striking and adventurous combinations. Depending on which way the sides of the tray are pulled together, its lining and outer fabric can be reversed to create different effects.

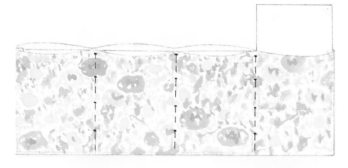
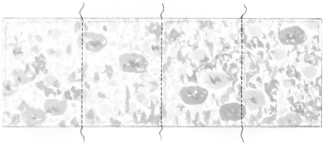

3 Inserting the cards Slip the first rectangle of stiff card between the two layers of fabric to lie next to one of the side seams. Make sure the card lies right up against the side seam, then hold it in place by running a line of pins through both layers of fabric, right next to the opposite edge of the card. Insert the other three card rectangles, holding them in place using pins in the same way; there should be a gap of roughly 5mm (¼in) between each card, with the last card lying against the second side seam.

4 Forming the sides Make sure that the cards are evenly spaced, then remove the pins at the top edge of the strip, fold in the long raw edges and glue or slipstitch the opening closed. Stitch down the channels between each card. Draw together the two ends of the strip and glue or stitch together to form a tube.

5 Making the base With right sides together and edges matching, stitch the two fabric squares together around three sides, taking a 1cm (½in) seam allowance. Trim seams, turn right side out and press. Insert square of card, turn in raw edges and slipstitch or glue closed. Glue or stitch base to tube, and trim with ribbon.

TISSUE-BOX COVER

The tissue-box cover is made in a similar way to the pot, but has a shaped top section and no base.

1 Cutting out Cut five pieces of card to fit sides and top of tissue box. From fabric, cut two rectangles the box height plus 2cm (1in), by the circumference of the box plus 3.5cm (1¾in), and one the same size as box top, plus 1cm (½in) all round.

2 Stitching the cover Follow steps 2, 3 and 4 of making the *Dressing-table pot* to make up a four-sided tube which fits over the tissue box. Trim the bottom of the tube with ribbon, as for the pot.

3 Shaping the top Take the pull-out piece of card from tissue-box top and centre it on remaining square of card. Trace around card pull-out, ensuring it is correctly positioned; cut away centre of card square.

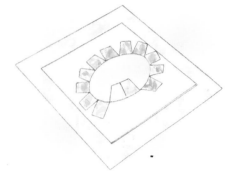

4 Sticking down the fabric Thinly apply glue to card square and stick centrally over remaining square of fabric. Make a small slit in the centre of the fabric, within the hole, and make small cuts out to sides of hole, stopping just before the edge. Smooth each section of fabric over edge of hole, and stick in place on the underside of the square of card.

5 Attaching the top Snip into the corners of the excess fabric around the box top. Apply glue to inside of the fabric-covered tube, around top edge. Stick top in place by gluing the excess fabric around it to the inside top rim of the tube.

Desk set

The smart desk set shown in the opening picture is made in a similar way to the dressing-table set, and shows the strikingly different effects that can be created through a change of fabric and decorative details.

To make the filing tray, simply follow the tray instructions already given. However, instead of inserting ribbon ties at each corner of the tray, attach loops and buttons (see step 2 below) to creat a classically elegant, tailored effect.

Materials

Stiff card to make up the containers. (See instructions for quantities.)
Fabric to cover the containers – use a contrast fabric to line the inside. (See instructions for quantities.)
Grosgrain ribbon 12mm (½in) wide to match the fabrics; you will need about 1m (40in)
Five buttons
Matching sewing threads
Rubber-solution adhesive

NOTELET HOLDER

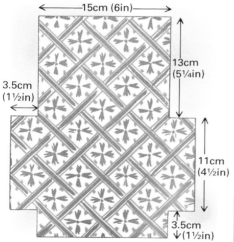

1 Cutting out From the stiff card, cut out two rectangles measuring 13 x 9cm (5 x 3½in), two strips measuring 13 x 3cm (5 x 1¼in), and two strips measuring 9 x 3cm (3½ x 1¼in). From both your main and lining fabric, cut out a piece to the shape and dimensions shown in the diagram.

► Take note

Fill your notelet holder with loose leaves of paper, cut to size, in a neutral shade or in a colour to match their container. To complete the desk set, you can also easily cover your diary, appointment or address book with matching fabric.

2 Attaching the ribbons Cut two 17cm (7in) lengths of grosgrain ribbon. Measure 11cm (4½in) down from the top of your main piece of fabric, and mark at both side edges (this part of the fabric piece will be the lid of the box). Stick down the two lengths of ribbon, extending them from the marked points to the top of the fabric piece, and crossing them over just below the edge, as shown. Cut a third, shorter length of ribbon and fold to form a loop. Tack ends to the top edge of the fabric piece, just above where the ribbons cross. Trim the ribbon ends to lie level with the edge of the fabric.

3 Stitching the tray With right sides together and edges matching, place the second (lining) piece of fabric over the first. Taking a 1cm (½in) seam allowance, stitch around the edges of the fabric, leaving the bottom edge unstitched. Trim seam allowances, turn through to right side and press flat.

4 Inserting the cards Position the card pieces and stitch each one in place as for the *Dressing-table tray*, beginning with the lid (**a**), then the long strip below the lid (**b**), then the two shorter side strips (**c** and **d**), followed by the base (**e**) and finally the long front strip (**f**). Fold in the raw edges and slipstitch or glue closed.

5 Forming the box Draw together the ends of the four card strips and slipstitch or glue them together to form the box. Stitch a button to the front of the box, positioning it where the loop falls.

Basket bows

F abric bows are just right for decorating useful but otherwise uninspiring baskets and boxes and if you stiffen them with glue like these, they will last longer and keep their shape. Use fabrics left over from your home furnishings or choose contrasting extravagant prints that will complement your home. Since each bow takes very little fabric you can afford to buy it off the roll or use bargain remnants. Choose fresh spring and summer prints for a really refreshing look or strong colours for a striking effect.

Cotton and cotton/polyester are excellent fabrics to use as they are fairly absorbent, firm enough to hold the bow shapes and soft enough to gather. Avoid thick, bulky fabrics and fabrics that fray easily, as both types are difficult to work with. Making these stiffened bows is really easy as PVA glue is transparent

▲ Take a bow
Plain baskets are given a finishing touch by the addition of charming bows. Choose colours that co-ordinate with the room you are going to place the finished basket in.

when it dries and the treated fabric stays pliable for several hours, allowing you to shape, and if necessary remodel, the bows.

Materials

Basket with handle
Cotton fabric remnant 20 x 140cm (8 x 54in) for each bow
PVA glue one bottle
Basin for mixing the glue
Egg cup to use as a measure
Paint brush 2.5cm (1in)
Fabric scissors
Florists' wire
Pencil and **ruler**
Tape measure and **pins**
Kitchen foil

STIFFENING THE BOWS

1 Preparing the glue mix Using the egg cup as a measure, mix two parts water to eight of glue. Stir well.

2 Cutting fabric into strips Measure around the basket and add on 5cm (2in) to the measurement. Decide on the width of this band, double the measurement and add 2cm (¾in). Cut a strip of fabric to this size. Wrap the tape measure around the basket handle for measurement, add 5cm (2in) then cut out a strip of fabric this length by 8cm (3in) wide.

Alternative bows

When attaching bows to items such as boxes with solid sides, omit the second length of wire and use undiluted PVA to secure them in place. For a double bow, make two fabric rings and gather up together. You could cut the bow ends at an angle and tuck the raw edges under for a neater finish.

3 Preparing the fabric strips Fold over 1cm (⅜in) to wrong side around both strips and press. Then fold strips in half lengthways with wrong sides together and press once more. Pass each fabric band through the glue mix pushing it down into the liquid with the paint brush. Run the fabric strip through your fingers to remove any excess glue; stick wrong sides together to form a neat strip.

4 Attaching the bands Decide on the best position for the bow, then beginning and ending at this point, wrap the first fabric band around the basket. Scrunch the ends to make them narrower, then pin in place. If necessary tuck and pin the band so that it hugs the basket. Wrap the second fabric band spirally around the handle, neatly tucking under the ends. Pin, then leave in a warm room to dry; remove pins.

5 Measuring for the main bow Using the tape measure decide on the size of the bow. Cut out a strip twice the length (**A**) plus 6cm (2¼in) by twice the width (**B**) plus 2cm (¾in). Cut a second strip for the ties measuring the bow length (**A**) plus 8cm (3in) by twice the width (**B**) plus 2cm (¾in). Cut a third strip for the knot 15 x 6cm (6 x 2¼in).

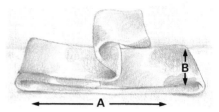

6 Making the bow Fold 1cm (⅜in) to wrong side around all the fabric pieces and press, fold strips in half lengthways with wrong sides together and press once again. Completely cover the fabric bow pieces with the glue mix as before. Overlap the longer strip by 4cm (1¾in) to form a ring. With the join on top in the centre, flatten the ring then lay the second tie-strip on top.

7 Gathering up the bow Cut two 14cm (5½in) lengths of wire and lay one piece of wire across the back of the bow. Wrap the remaining piece of wire around the centre of the bow to gather it up, then twist the ends to fasten; trim wire ends.

8 Completing the bow Coat one side of the third strip with undiluted PVA, then wrap around the gathered part of the bow ending at the back; trim ends if necessary. Arrange the bow into shape, then stuff bow loops with scrunched foil to help them hold their shape. Leave in a warm room until thoroughly dry checking bows regularly to be sure that they maintain their shape.

9 Making the handle bow Make a smaller bow for the basket handle as for the larger bow using the tape measure to check the proportions before cutting the fabric.

10 Attaching the bows Using the paintbrush, coat underside of each bow with undiluted PVA. Bend the wire ends at right angles to the bow and insert through the basket, twist the ends to secure, then trim.

Fabric-covered plates

Fabric-covered plates, grouped together on a wall, make a magnificent display. They are also a perfect way of giving odd or slightly damaged plates a new lease of life while showing off your favourite scraps of fabric.

If you do not have any scraps around the house, buy remnants especially for the purpose to make a collection that co-ordinates. Cover flat or shallow plates only and pick round or oval shapes, you will find plates with corners or shaped edges difficult to cover.

If you are going to use a light coloured fabric, choose either a white plate or one with a pale pattern. Closely woven dress or furnishing fabrics that are light to medium-weight, non-stretch and do not fray easily are ideal for plate covering.

If you have recently made curtains or have had some soft covers made use any remaining fabric to cover some plates, then organise your collection of remnants around these to create a look that will complete the room.

Materials
Plate flat or shallow
Dress or **furnishing fabric** 15cm (6in) larger all round than plate
PVA glue
Paint brush 2.5cm (1in) wide
Jam jar or **bowl** for glue
Scissors
Soft pencil
Mug, jam jar or **flower pot** for stand

▲ *Exact match*
On close inspection you can see that these unusual plates are covered with furnishing fabrics. Friends will find it amazing that you have managed to find plates to match your soft furnishings exactly.

COVERING A PLATE

1 Cutting the fabric Working on a flat, washable surface, smooth the fabric out and position the plate face down on to the fabric, framing any motifs or section of pattern you wish to show off. Using the pencil lightly draw a line around the plate leaving a border the width of the plate from rim to centre. Using scissors, cut along the drawn line.

2 Pasting the fabric Add 1 part of water to 2 parts of PVA in a jar and stir until mixed. Using the brush, paint glue mix over the top of the plate. Lay fabric, wrong side down, centrally over the plate and smooth the fabric from the centre outwards. Paint another layer of glue over the fabric and smooth out, pressing well into the contours of the plate.

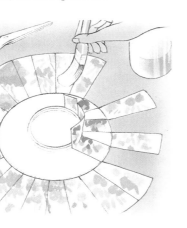

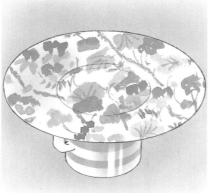

3 Neaten the fabric allowance Turn the plate over and cut the fabric allowance almost up to the plate edge, at 2.5cm (1in) intervals. Paint glue mix over the back of the plate and wrong side of each fabric allowance section. Press each alternate section to the back of the plate, working around until all the flaps are in place. Brush another layer of paste over the surface and smooth the fabric sections again.

4 Checking for air bubbles Turn the plate over and check fabric is still smooth. Press out any air bubbles and dampen with another coat of glue mix if necessary.

▲ Floral threesome
To co-ordinate remnant-covered plates, choose fabrics with a distinct linking theme such as a colour or a motif like these three flower prints.

5 Trimming the fabric When the plate is finished, trim away any excess fabric to make a neat circle at the back. Balance the plate on the stand and leave to dry for at least twelve hours.

Treasure troves

If you have a prize collection of trinkets or memorabilia hidden away in the back of a drawer or cupboard, now is just the time to sort it out and set it into a pleasing and delightful display using these pretty boxes.

The boxes are sold unfinished giving you the opportunity to paint them in a colour to match your collection or decor. They can be treated in a variety of ways to add a touch of colour to the wood. A specialist liming wax was used to give the wood on one box a pale, but interesting sheen. The green box was given a wash of wood glaze to colour the wood but still preserve its interesting grain. The final box was simply but vigorously buffed

with a traditional furniture wax in order to creat a warm brown veneer with a deep and lasting shine.

Besides colouring the box to match the collection try to match the finish of each box with its surroundings as well. Once decorated, boxes destined for the kitchen or bathroom should be finished with a protective coat of varnish, while a coat of wax is sufficient for boxes which will live in other rooms.

Once the box is dry, add the display. Collections of shells, flowers, herbs and seeds can all be used either fitting just one in each compartment or by tightly packing each division. If you wish, once you are happy with the arrangement,

▲ A place for everything
These delightful boxes with their separate compartments are perfect for displaying all your small trinkets and favourite treasures. If you don't have a complete collection of curiosities yet, leave some of the spaces free ready to display special items as they arrive.

you can also glue the pieces of your collection in place thus ensuring that each piece stays in its compartment. These boxes will be a unique alternative to pictures or framed embroideries and provide a happy memory of holidays and special occasions.

LIMING A BOX WITH WAX

Materials

Wooden display box 23cm (9in) square
Stiff wire brush
Liming wax Available at home improvement stores
Steel wool
Furniture wax
Rubber gloves and **clean rags**

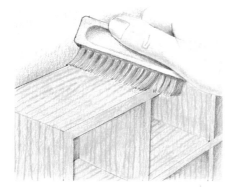

1 Preparing the box Raise the grain of the box with a stiff wire brush. Wipe away any dust with a damp cloth and leave to dry.

2 Liming the box Wearing rubber gloves and following the manufacturers' instructions, liberally coat all the surfaces with liming wax. Working with a small pad of steel wool rub it against the wood grain to make sure all the indentations are liberally filled and coloured white.

3 Working the wax Begin with the box partitions then work the wax and wool round the box inside and out. Renew the wool pad as it becomes clogged with wax.

4 Removing excess lime When the wax is dry, coat all limed surfaces with furniture wax using a clean rag, rubbing vigorously to remove the excess liming wax. Keep moving to a clean area of the rag as it becomes clogged with lime.

5 Buff the wax When you have worked over the box both inside and out, buff the wax with a clean soft cotton cloth to produce a soft sheen. Re-wax when necessary to protect or renew the shine.

STAINING A BOX

Materials

Wooden display box 15cm (6in) square
Woodwash wood stain in conifer
Flat or **matt varnish**
Artists' brush
Rubber gloves
Clean rag
Paint brush

1 Staining the inside Wearing rubber gloves, begin staining each partition individually using the artists' brush to reach the inner corners. Wipe away excess stain with a clean rag as you work. Complete the inside of the box before working on the outside.

2 Staining the outside Use a clean rag to stain the outer surfaces. Press lightly and evenly to apply a thin coat of stain over the surfaces. Work in the same direction as the grain, and work quickly. Wipe over with a clean cloth to pick up excess stain. Allow to dry.

3 Add a second coat Once dry, if the stain looks too thin, apply a second coat in the same way and leave to dry.

4 Applying varnish When dry, protect the box by applying a coat of matt varnish, working with a small paint brush. Leave to dry thoroughly.

Using stain
It's easier to decant some of the wood stain into a saucer before starting work. Strip the wood before applying a new finish.

Waxing a box
Wearing rubber gloves, rub wax liberally on to all the surfaces. Begin inside the box with the box divisions and push the cloth well into the corners to coat them with wax. Work wax over the outside of the box in the same way always working in the direction of the wood grain, until a deep even coat of wax has been applied. Leave to dry. Once dry, use another clean cloth to buff the box to a deep sheen. Repeat the process as necessary, until the overall effect and colour tone is as desired.

Painted pottery

Plain pottery with low relief designs can be given completely new and colourful looks with ceramic paints. The painting technique is really easy because the raised motifs on the pottery have clearly marked outlines, so any budding artists can try their hand without worrying about their lack of artistic skills. Glazed white or cream ware with border designs of fruit and flowers make excellent subjects for this decorative effect, and you can select colours to complement your decor. Buy your plates and bowls from major department stores because these are inexpensive, or buy reproductions of antique designs.

Design options

When selecting pottery designs to paint, decide how you would like to use the colours. You can paint the motifs in a natural way, adding shadows and tonal changes, or you can aim for a more stylized, dramatic effect. Consider different approaches too; you can reserve the colour for the raised motifs, leaving the background plain, or you can paint part of this to blend or contrast with the main design.

Look at each piece to decide what elements could be painted to complement the main motif – perhaps even a

▼ Mix and match
Complement your colour scheme with hand-painted pottery. Give each piece an individual look with different colour rims, but balance the effect with matching painted motifs.

▲ Brushstrokes
Add interest to large plain areas with paint and an almost dry brush.

coloured border, or a handle could add the right touch. If you are painting several pieces in a set you can ring the changes by altering the colour sequence on each piece; a border on a plate can be picked out in one colour, to contrast with the border on a bowl or smaller plate. Completely different designs can also be linked with colour in this way.

Safety features
When using ceramic paints, always follow the manufacturer's instructions closely. Many paints are non-toxic, but regulations specify that ceramic paints and their protective varnishes should not be in direct contact with the mouth or food, so painted pottery is best reserved for decorative use only.

Using ceramic paints
There are two main types of ceramic paints – water-based paints and solvent-based paints. The water-based paints are very durable, but the painted pottery has to be baked at a high temperature in an oven, so a sample test should be tried first. The solvent-based paints are easier to use, they require no baking and will withstand gentle washing. The finished designs should be protected with a paint-on glaze available from the paint manufacturers, or with a clear polyurethane varnish.

Materials
White glazed pottery with relief design
Solvent-based paints in a range of colours
White spirit for thinning colours and cleaning brushes
Brushes fine and medium point and flat watercolour brushes
Glaze or **clear polyurethane varnish**
Old plate to use as palette for colour mixing
Paper tissues and **cotton buds** for drying brushes and mopping up paint spills

PAINTING THE DESIGNS

1 Preparing the surface The pottery should be clean and dry. Choose the most prominent motif for the first colour and paint all these shapes. Working this way will help you to balance the colours. Apply the paint economically, keeping just within the design outline so a little of the background colour is visible between the motifs. Use the paint sparingly so the translucent brush strokes echo the raised design.

2 Working the next colour Paint the second colour using the same method. Choose a part of the design not touching the first colour, to minimise the risk of colour-runs. If these occur, dab a cotton bud in white spirit to wipe the area. Use a dry bud to blot and clean away colour residue.

3 Painting details Avoid working close to wet areas wherever possible. Use dark and light shades of one colour when painting massed groups like leaves, clusters of berries, petals etc, to add depth and contrast to the design.

4 Adding brush effects These can be used for colouring-in subtle raised areas where the design is indistinct, and to add colour interest to rims and handles. Use them on large areas too, where no solid relief pattern divides the design – on the centres of plates or dishes for example. Dry brush strokes give a softer effect than a solid painted line, and are easier to control.

5 Working with a dry brush To create these effects, dab excess paint from a flat brush and lightly stroke the brush over the required area. If painting a rim, support the object in one hand and work round the shape, turning the object as you brush. When re-loading with colour, gently brush the paint in to blend with the other brush strokes.

6 Finishing the work Leave the paint to dry for 24 hours, then paint over the surface with a thin layer of glaze or household varnish. Leave until completely dry.

▼ Borderlines
Highlight design features with colours to match the main motif.